GW00467549

The Essential Greek Cookbook

A Gastronomic Journey through the Land of Gods
and Olives with an Abundance of Authentic,
Delicious, and Easy Greek Recipes.

Author: Sophia Katsaros

Table of Contents

4

A Taste Of History And Tradition Of The Greek Kitchen

It won't surprise you to learn that Greek cooking has a long history, and that we can trace the Greek culinary arts back to around 320 B.C., when the first known Greek cookbook was written by the poet Archestratus. Although things have of course changed, many of the fundamentals of Greek cooking have remained the same to this day, and it's amazing to see what a rich history this style of cooking has.

Greek food is known for being delicious, healthy, light, and full of flavour. Olive oil is most commonly associated with this style of cuisine, and for good reason; it's at the heart of most of the dishes. It's also considered super healthy and tasty, which is part of what has made Greek cooking popular over the years.

Greek cooking also includes a lot of grains, vegetables, seasonal fruits, and fish. Meat is used, but it's not as pervasive in Greek cuisine as in some other kinds of cooking. A lot more is eaten today than was used in the past, when meat was mostly saved for ceremonies and special days. It's considered a frugal diet, and is very much a part of Mediterranean cooking.

Spices and herbs are used abundantly, and Greek food tends to be more heavily flavoured than some kinds of Mediterranean cuisine. Sweet spices are frequently paired with meats, while the savoury spices appear alongside vegetables and fish. Wine is the main accompaniment for Greek food, and this cuisine is among the best-known and tastiest options out there.

When Greece was taken over by the Romans, Roman cuisine somewhat influenced Greek cooking, and around 330 A.D., with the founding of the Byzantine Empire, Byzantine cuisine also brought new ingredients, including things like lemons, nutmeg, caviar, and basil. Many of these ingredients are now prominent in Greek cooking, even though they may not have been "original."

There's also a lot of overlap with Italian cooking, thanks to the proximity of the two countries. Greek food has absorbed influences from other parts of the world too, leading to a rich and varied style of eating that is enjoyed by people across the globe.

Greeks are very proud of their cuisine, and for good reason. If you visit Greece, you will find you have a vast range of dining options, with superb meals and an enormous amount of choice on offer.

Some of the top Greek dishes include:

- Rusks: these are made with barley flour and double-baked; they are delicious and are usually topped with olive oil and feta cheese

- Pastitsio: somewhat like lasagna, this is layers of pasta, tomato, and bechamel

- Spanakopita: this is a delicious spinach-stuffed pie, incorporating filo pastry, eggs, herbs, and feta cheese

- Saganaki: this is a fried cheese, usually used as an appetiser

- Fava: this is a creamy puree made from fava beans or yellow split peas, and is often used as a dip

- Souvlaki: for this dish, meats such as lamb, pork, and chicken are cooked on skewers and may be eaten as they are or in pita breads

- Baklava: this is a traditional sweet made with filo pastry, chopped nuts, and honey

- Tzatziki: this is a cold dip made using garlic, dill, Greek yoghurt, lemon juice, and cucumbers

- Moussaka: this is a layered casserole that incorporates vegetables like aubergines, garlic, onions, tomatoes, and spices, plus a bechamel topping

- Stifado: this dish was traditionally made with rabbit, but sometimes uses beef, alongside tomatoes, onions, and spices

It's worth noting that although "Greek cuisine" is a concept, the foods do vary from region to region, and some dishes will only be found in certain areas. In Central Greece and the North-West, the dishes tend to include a lot of filo. A lot of other dishes are served countrywide, but the ingredients and cooking style will vary by region.

It's important to understand that the Greek people have a deep and lasting respect for food. Ingredients are often sourced locally and are of high quality, and people treat food with love. In many places, communal eating was the norm, and even today, many Greek dishes are based on shared dips, vegetables, appetisers, etc. Greek people eat out a lot, and meals are seen as an important opportunity to share time with family members and take a pause in the chaos of everyday life.

With all that in mind, it's no surprise that Greek cuisine is so popular. It brings together simple but delicious food, good health and nutrition, and high-quality, flavourful ingredients that are combined with love, history, and respect.

Essential Greek Ingredients And Greek Pantry Must-Haves For Exploring Greek Cuisine

It's important to know what kinds of ingredients you're likely to be making use of in your Greek cooking adventures. You will probably want to stock up on the core ingredients, especially if you haven't done a lot of Mediterranean cooking before.

Having some of the most important ingredients to hand can make life easier, and will allow you to enrich your cooking and make truly mouth-watering dishes every time you cook.

With that in mind, let's look at the things you need most to start making Greek food! Some of the top ingredients include things like:

- Olive oil: as already mentioned, this is a staple of Greek food and is found in a vast array of dishes.

- Olives: it's not just the oil; olives are found in so many Greek dishes, it would be impossible to list them. They are stuffed, added to salads, found in marinades, and eaten plain.

- Greek honey: an ancient form of sweetener, this is present in many Greek desserts and in some meals as well.

- Fish and seafood: fish is another Greek staple, especially near the coast, and octopus is regularly eaten too. Greece is bordered by the sea on two sides, so it makes sense that many dishes would revolve around seafood. Mussels are another common option.

- Oregano: many Greek dishes call for oregano, including salads, marinades, kebabs, roasted potatoes, and more.

- Mint: mint is used in a lot of stews, including lamb stew, and marinades, as well as certain beverages.

- Basil: commonly used alongside tomato, basil is another very popular herb in Greek cooking. Fresh basil is particularly aromatic and delicious, but you can use dried if you have to.

- Thyme: you need thyme for the warmer Greek dishes, like roast chicken, and for garlicky soups, plus some stews.

- Garlic: so many Greek dishes use garlic, you'll want to stock up. Get fresh garlic, rather than powdered.

- Lemons: although they were added to the cuisine later, lemons are a vital part of a lot of

Greek recipes today, and you'll find that you're squeezing them into dressings, across potatoes, and over grilled meat constantly.

- Feta cheese: as the national Greek cheese, it won't surprise you see to feta in a lot of dishes, although it is only produced in certain regions.

- Mastic: an ingredient that many people will not even have heard of, mastic is used in a lot of Greek cooking. It's crystallised resin that comes from the pistachio tree, and it's used in both sweet and savoury dishes.

- Fruits: fruit is a big aspect of Greek cuisine as well, and is usually eaten according to the season. Fresh fruits are used in lots of recipes, or eaten just as they are.

- Yoghurt: Greek yoghurt is famous and is used in many dishes to lend them a creamy, rich flavour.

- Legumes: legumes like chickpeas, beans, peas, etc., are the base of a lot of Greek meals, and they make dishes filling without needing meat or fat.

- Capers: capers are usually pickled in Western cuisine, and they are thought to be very healthy. They can be baked with wine and herbs to make a really flavourful snack, or as part of a bigger dish.

How To Prepare Mouthwatering Appetisers And Dips

There are lots of ways to make incredible appetisers and dips, and these are a large part of Greek cuisine. Because the food is often eaten communally, shared dips and shared appetisers are a big part of many meals, and much of the joy of Greek cooking is combining lots of flavours and textures.

It's a good idea to practise making a combination of different appetisers, so you have lots of options to turn to. It may take a little while to learn all the recipes, but it will be worth it, because this will expand your repertoire and give your meals a truly authentic Greek feeling.

Greek appetisers and dips include things like:

- Greek layer dip, which is made with black olives, feta cheese, cucumbers, hummus, and tomatoes

- Stuffed cucumber bites, which involve scooping the pulp out of the cucumber and putting red onions, feta cheese, olives, and tomatoes in the hollowed space.

- Saganaki, which involves rolling cheese in flour and frying it until it's deliciously golden and crispy

- Tzatziki garlic dip, which is made with Greek yoghurt, fresh cucumber, garlic, dill, and lemon.

- Salad skewers, which are usually created with tomatoes, cucumber, black olives, and cheese chunks.

- Meatballs, which come in a variety of flavours and styles, and are often served with dips.

- Filo pastry parcels, which can have a whole range of fillings and are delicious little bites of crunchy pastry and vegetables.

- Meze platters, which are a little like a Greek charcuterie, combining things like peppers, bread, olives, cheese, and dips.

- Olive tapenade, which is a blend of capers, olives, olive oil, and anchovies, and tends to be spread on bread.

You can make some of these amazing Greek appetisers in advance, and this is a great way of ensuring you get a nice variety with every meal. Simply refrigerate dips, meatballs, and other similar options, and then pull them out (and heat them if appropriate) when mealtime rolls around.

Some things, of course, can't easily be made much in advance. Appetisers that contain filo pastry are usually best made as fresh as possible, so that the pastry remains light and flaky.

You can keep filo pastry items for up to a week, but be aware that they may be softer and less enjoyable as a result. You can also freeze filo pastry and reheat it in the oven to refresh it, which works well.

One of the most important things to bear in mind when it comes to making great Greek appetisers is that it's okay to customise them to your preferences. Greek food is full of variation, and there's no single "right" way to make something, so try different things and find what works out best for you. You'll enjoy much more success if you're flexible with your recipes, and happy to experiment a bit.

Remember that the key to truly mouthwatering appetisers and dips is to use high-quality ingredients and maximise the flavour as much as possible. Where you can, get fresh vegetables, and consider making your own filo pastry if you have the time. Making your own dips is a great idea too, even if they're just one component of the appetiser.

This will ensure you have delicious, fresh, and ultra-tasty appetisers, and ensures you can tailor things to suit your exact tastes. It's also often healthier, as ready-made foods generally have unnecessary salt, sugar, and other preservatives in them. As often as possible, freshly homemade is the best option for great-tasting food!

Essential Tips And Techniques For Mastering Greek Cooking

You will be pleased to learn that a lot of Greek cooking is very straightforward, and uses techniques you are probably already familiar with. However, here are a few tips that will help you to master Greek cooking.

Tip 1) Learn the techniques

Frying, sautéing, boiling, simmering, braising, roasting, stewing, baking, pickling, poaching, and stewing all come into this kind of cuisine, which means it's easy to get into making this sort of meal, especially if you're already familiar with these kinds of techniques.

If you're not, it's worth practising them a bit with some basic ingredients – for example, have a go at poaching an egg, before you try a complicated meal that involves poaching fish. Remember that a lot of skills are transferable, so once you've learned a technique, you'll be able to use it in lots of ways.

Tip 2) Learn the spices

Learning how to use the most popular spices is one of the best ways to help yourself out when it comes to Greek cooking. Herbs and spices are used to enrich dishes, and while experimenting can be great, it's also good to know what combinations tend to work well and what you should opt for.

The below may help you out a bit when it comes to flavouring meats and fish:

- Fish goes well with pepper, marjoram, dill, and curry powder

- Pork goes well with garlic, onion, rosemary, pepper, oregano, and sage

- Chicken goes well with sage, rosemary, paprika, oregano, ginger, sage, thyme, marjoram, and curry powder

- Beef goes well with nutmeg, pepper, tarragon, onion, thyme, and bay leaves

- Lamb goes well with mint, garlic, curry, rosemary, and cumin

Tip 3) Experiment with flavours

Greek cooking often involves experimenting, and may require you to tap into some bold flavours. This food is not generally mild, and it's fine to try new things.

Use things like lemon and Greek yoghurt to bump up the sharpness or creaminess of your dishes, and spend some time familiarising yourself with the humble tomato – one of the centrepieces of all Mediterranean cooking.

Don't be afraid of trying new combinations and increasing or decreasing the herbs and spices as you adapt to Greek cooking. There's no "wrong" way to do this; just find the flavours you love, and use them to make your food taste exceptional.

Tip 4) Make in advance

It's important to remember that you don't have to make everything fresh when it comes to Greek food; it's okay to have some make-ahead recipes that you keep in the fridge and whip out when you're ready to eat.

Because Greek food often has side dishes and dips, this can reduce the risk of you feeling overwhelmed by having to make lots of individual dishes every time you cook. Make extra, refrigerate it, and pull it out to go with your main course.

Tip 5) Learn to marinate

It's also a good idea to learn how to marinate foods, as this is another key aspect of getting those rich flavours you're looking for.

Soaking ingredients like tofu, meats, and fish in marinades can create the real depth that a lot of Mediterranean cooking is famous for – but if you're not used to marinating foods, you may need to practise a little, as this involves leaving extra time for the meal prep. It's not hands-on time so it's not particularly hard, but it does involve being a little more organised than usual.

Tip 6) Use fresh and properly-stored ingredients

As mentioned above, the fresher the ingredient, the better the meal will taste. Fresh ingredients, especially when it comes to herbs and vegetables, are important for truly mastering Greek cooking. Dried herbs and older vegetables just don't taste the same.

Check out your local farmers' markets, or consider getting delivery from a local company to make the most of fresh food. It will taste better, and be better for you!

It's also important to learn how to correctly store your ingredients to make sure they taste as good as possible.

Check out top storage tips for the ingredients you're going to be using, and you may find you've been storing them wrongly for years.

For example, many people are not aware that you shouldn't put your tomatoes in the fridge. This destroys the flavour, and makes the tomatoes taste bland and dull. Instead, keep tomatoes in a cool, dark place, such as a pantry shelf.

Always check how to store something when you buy it, and your food will have a much better flavour!

Resources And Recommendations For Further Greek Culinary Exploration

This book is filled with tasty recipes that will open up the world of Greek cooking and introduce you to all sorts of new dishes – but don't stop here! There's still so much more to learn.

You might want to consider taking a course in Greek cooking; these may be available near you, and you will learn an enormous amount from working with an authentic Greek chef who can guide you and show you all the tricks of the trade. You will also meet other enthusiasts, who can inspire you, teach you, and learn from you.

If you don't have classes available nearby or you don't fancy this option, you could consider following blogs, YouTube channels, celebrity chefs, or just online recipes to explore Greek cooking and learn more about it. You'll find lots of helpful tips for cooking, and one of the beauties of the internet is that you can connect with real Greek chefs while you do it.

You should also consider looking at other kinds of Mediterranean cuisine, which is a great way to expand your thinking and encourage yourself to experiment and learn more about this kind of food. Because there's a lot of overlap between Greek cooking and other kinds of Mediterranean cooking, you can expand your repertoire and learn new techniques and flavour combinations with this method.

Food from Morocco, Italy, Portugal, Spain, Turkey, France, and Egypt is generally considered Mediterranean, so spend a bit of time exploring these cuisines and getting to know what different techniques and combinations of flavours they use.

You might want to pick up some cookbooks that focus on other kinds of Mediterranean cooking, especially once you've exhausted this book. If you're still enthusiastic and you want to learn more, there are lots of options and resources out there!

With all that in mind, let's get started on some great Greek recipes so you can begin your journey with Greek cuisine.

Breakfast Recipes

Strawberry Oatmeal Smoothie

Servings | 2   Time | 10 minutes
Nutritional Content (per serving):
Cal | 227   Fat | 4g   Protein | 10g   Carbs | 37.9g   Fibre | 5.1g

Ingredients:

- ❖ 190 grams (1½ cups) frozen strawberries
- ❖ 25 grams (¼ cup) old-fashioned oats
- ❖ 180 millilitres (¾ cup) unsweetened almond milk
- ❖ 1 medium-sized banana, peel removed and sliced
- ❖ 250 grams (1 cup) plain Greek yogurt

Directions:

1. In a high-power mixer, put in strawberries and remnant ingredients and process to form a smooth and creamy mixture.
2. Enjoy immediately.

Banana & Yogurt Smoothie

Servings | 2   Time | 10 minutes
Nutritional Content (per serving):
Cal | 191   Fat | 3g   Protein | 5.5g   Carbs | 36.6g   Fibre | 4g

Ingredients:

- ❖ 2 large-sized bananas, peel removed and sliced
- ❖ 240 millilitres (1 cup) unsweetened almond milk
- ❖ 5 millilitres (1 teaspoon) vanilla extract
- ❖ 125 grams (½ cup) plain Greek yogurt

Directions:

1. In a high-power mixer, put in bananas and remnant ingredients and process to form a smooth and creamy mixture.
2. Enjoy immediately.

Yogurt Bowl with Figs

Servings | 4   Time | 15 minutes
Nutritional Content (per serving):
Cal | 296   Fat | 3.8g   Protein | 9.7g   Carbs | 58.8g   Fibre | 6g

Ingredients:

- ❖ 60 grams (3 tablespoons) honey, divided
- ❖ 500 grams (2 cups) plain Greek yogurt
- ❖ 225 grams (8 ounces) fresh figs, halved
- ❖ 65 grams (¼ cup) pistachios, cut up

Directions:

1. In a medium-sized wok, put in 20 grams (1 tablespoon) of honey on burner at around medium heat.
2. Cook for around 1-2 minutes.
3. In the wok, put in figs, cut sides down and cook for around 5 minutes.
4. Take off the wok of figs from burner and put it aside for around 2-3 minutes.
5. Divide the yogurt into serving dishes and top each with the caramelized fig halves.
6. Sprinkle with pistachios.
7. Drizzle each dish with remnant honey and enjoy.

Fruity Yogurt Parfait

Servings | 4   Time | 25 minutes
Nutritional Content (per serving):
Cal | 255   Fat | 5.1g   Protein | 14.7g   Carbs | 39.1g   Fibre | 2g

Ingredients:

- ❖ 500 grams (2 cups) plain Greek yogurt
- ❖ 60 millilitres (¼ cup) water
- ❖ 2½ grams (½ teaspoon) lemon zest, grated finely
- ❖ 2 peaches, pitted and quartered
- ❖ 4 plums, pitted and quartered
- ❖ 60 grams (¼ cup) honey, divided
- ❖ 25 grams (2 tablespoons) sugar
- ❖ 1¼ grams (¼ teaspoon) ground cinnamon
- ❖ 1¼ millilitres (¼ teaspoon) vanilla extract
- ❖ 25 grams (¼ cup) almonds, toasted and cut up

Directions:

1. In a large-sized basin, put in yogurt and honey and blend to incorporate thoroughly. Put it aside.
2. In a saucepan, blend all together water, sugar, lemon zest, cinnamon and vanilla extract on burner at around medium heat.
3. Blend in peaches and plums and cook for around 8-10 minutes, mixing time to time.
4. Take off from burner and put it aside to cool thoroughly.
5. Divide half of the yogurt mixture in four tall serving glasses.
6. Divide the fruit mixture over yogurt.
7. Place remnant yogurt over fruit mixture
8. Decorate with almonds and enjoy.

Eggs, Spinach & Tomato Scramble

Servings | 2   Time | 20 minutes
Nutritional Content (per serving):
Cal | 201   Fat | 16.5g   Protein | 11g   Carbs | 2.8g   Fibre | 0.7g

Ingredients:

- ❖ 15 millilitres (1 tablespoon) olive oil
- ❖ 75 grams (1/3 cup) tomato, cut up
- ❖ 15 grams (2 tablespoons) feta cheese, cubed

- ❖ 30 grams (1 cup) fresh baby spinach
- ❖ 3 eggs, whisked
- ❖ Salt and powdered black pepper, as desired

Directions:

1. In a large-sized frying pan, sizzle oil on burner at around medium heat.
2. Put in spinach and tomatoes and cook for around 3-4 minutes.
3. Put in eggs and cook for around 1 minute, mixing all the time.
4. Blend in feta and cook for around 2 minutes.
5. Blend in salt and pepper and take off from burner.
6. Enjoy immediately.

Potato Omelet

Servings | 4   Time | 25 minutes
Nutritional Content (per serving):
Cal | 347   Fat | 29.8g   Protein | 7.6g   Carbs | 15.7g   Fibre | 3.1g

Ingredients:

- ❖ 60 millilitres (¼ cup) olive oil
- ❖ Salt and powdered black pepper, as desired
- ❖ 1 large-sized onion, thinly sliced
- ❖ 2 tomatoes, peel removed, seeded and roughly cut up
- ❖ 225 grams (½ pound) potatoes, thinly sliced
- ❖ 4 eggs
- ❖ 2 green onions, cut up

Directions:

1. In a large-sized wok, sizzle the oil on burner at around medium-high heat.
2. Cook the potatoes with a little salt and pepper for around 3-4 minutes.
3. Blend in onion and cook for around 5 minutes, mixing time to time.
4. Meanwhile, in a basin, put in eggs, salt and pepper and whisk to incorporate thoroughly.
5. Put in eggs mixture into the wok with potato mixture and gently, blend to incorporate.
6. Immediately turn down the heat at around low and cook until eggs begin to set on the bottom.
7. With a spatula, flip the omelet and cook until eggs are set.
8. Enjoy warm with the decoration of tomato and green onion.

Mixed Veggie Omelet

Servings|4   Time|30 minutes
Nutritional Content (per serving):
Cal| 208   Fat| 13.8g   Protein| 14.1g   Carbs| 8g   Fibre| 2.7g

Ingredients:

- ❖ 5 millilitres (1 teaspoon) olive oil
- ❖ 45 grams (¼ cup) canned artichoke hearts, rinsed, liquid removed and cut up
- ❖ 1 Roma tomato, cut up
- ❖ 6 eggs
- ❖ 55 grams (½ cup) goat cheese, crumbled
- ❖ 180 grams (2 cups) fresh fennel bulb, sliced thinly
- ❖ 45 grams (¼ cup) green olives, pitted and cut up
- ❖ Salt and powdered black pepper, as desired

Directions:

1. For preheating: set your oven at 165 °C (325 °F).
2. In a large-sized ovenproof wok, sizzle the oil on medium-high heat.
3. Put in fennel bulb and cook for around 5 minutes.
4. Blend in artichoke, olives and tomato and cook for around 3 minutes.
5. Meanwhile in a basin, put in eggs, salt and pepper and whisk to incorporate thoroughly.
6. Place the egg mixture over veggie mixture and blend to incorporate.
7. Cook for around 2 minutes.
8. Sprinkle with the goat cheese and immediately, shift the wok into the oven.
9. Bake in your oven for around 5 minutes.
10. Take off the wok from oven and shift the omelet onto a platter.
11. Divide into four wedges and enjoy.

Omelet Casserole

Servings | 8   Time | 55 minutes
Nutritional Content (per serving):
Cal | 273   Fat | 15.7g   Protein | 17.9g   Carbs | 14.9g   Fibre | 6.8g

Ingredients:

- Olive oil baking spray
- 225 grams (8 ounces) fresh spinach
- 12 large-sized eggs
- 5 grams (1 tablespoon) fresh dill, cut up
- 5 grams (1 teaspoon) salt
- 140 grams (5 ounces) sun-dried tomato feta cheese, crumbled
- 115 millilitres 15 millilitres (1 tablespoon) olive oil
- 2 cloves garlic, finely cut up
- 480 millilitres (2 cups) whole milk
- 5 grams (1 teaspoon) dried oregano
- 5 grams (1 teaspoon) lemon pepper
- 340 grams (12 ounces) artichoke salad, liquid removed and cut up

Directions:

1. Lay out a rack in the center of oven.
2. For preheating: set your oven at 190 °C (375 °F).
3. Spray a baking pan with baking spray.
4. In an anti-sticking wok, sizzle oil on burner at around medium heat.
5. Cook the spinach and garlic for around 3 minutes.
6. Take off the wok of spinach from burner and put it aside.
7. Meanwhile, in a medium-sized basin, put in eggs, milk, herbs, lemon pepper and salt and whisk to incorporate thoroughly.
8. Lay out the spinach and artichoke salad into the baking pan and top with egg mixture, followed by the feta cheese.
9. Bake in your oven for around 35-40 minutes.
10. Enjoy warm.

Yogurt Pancakes

Servings | 6   Time | 40 minutes
Nutritional Content (per serving):
Cal | 241   Fat | 9.1g   Protein | 10.1g   Carbs | 28.3g   Fibre | 2.3g

Ingredients:

- 65 grams (½ cup) all-purpose flour
- 20 grams (2 tablespoons) flaxseeds
- 1¼ grams (¼ teaspoon) salt
- 2 large-sized eggs
- 30 millilitres (2 tablespoons) olive oil
- 100 grams (1 cup) old-fashioned oats
- 4 grams (1 teaspoon) baking soda
- 40 grams (2 tablespoons) maple syrup
- 500 grams (2 cups) plain Greek yogurt

Directions:

1. In a high-power mixer, put in flour, oats, flax seeds, baking soda and salt and process to incorporate thoroughly.
2. Shift the blended mixture into a large-sized basin.
3. Put in remnant ingredients except for the oil and blend to incorporate thoroughly.
4. Put it aside for around 20 minutes before cooking.
5. In a large-sized anti-sticking wok, sizzle oil on burner at around medium heat.
6. Add desired amount of blended mixture and cook for around 2 minutes.
7. Carefully change the side and cook for around 2 minutes more.
8. Cook the remnant pancakes in the same method.
9. Enjoy warm.

Onion Pancakes

Servings|12   Time|1 hour 25 minutes
Nutritional Content (per serving):
Cal| 167   Fat| 4.6g   Protein| 3.8g   Carbs| 27.8g   Fibre| 1.9g

Ingredients:

- ❖ 60 millilitres (¼ cup) olive oil
- ❖ Salt, as desired
- ❖ 375 grams (3 cups) self-rising flour
- ❖ Powdered black pepper, as desired
- ❖ 480 grams (4 cups) onions, cut up
- ❖ 10 grams (½ cup) fresh mint, cut up
- ❖ 660 millilitres (2¾ cups) sparkling water
- ❖ Olive oil baking spray

Directions:

1. In a wok, sizzle oil on burner at around medium-low heat.
2. Cook the onions for around 2 minutes.
3. Stir the onions and cover the wok tightly.
4. Immediately turn down the heat very low and cook for around 20 minutes.
5. Take off from burner and blend in mint, a little salt and pepper.
6. Put it aside to cool for at least 15 minutes.
7. In a basin, put in flour, salt and water and blend to form a thick mixture.
8. Put in cooled onion mixture and pepper and gently blend to incorporate.
9. Lightly spray a heavy-bottomed cast-iron wok with baking spray and heat on burner at around medium-low heat.
10. Place desired amount of blended mixture and cook for around 2 minutes from both sides.
11. Cook the remnant pancakes in the same method.
12. Enjoy warm.

Dates & Prunes Muffins

Servings | 6   Time | 40 minutes
Nutritional Content (per serving):
Cal | 389   Fat | 17.2g   Protein | 5.6g   Carbs | 57.2g   Fibre | 4.4g

Ingredients:

- 240 millilitres (1 cup) water
- 90 grams (½ cup) prunes, pitted and cut up
- 115 grams (½ cup) butter, cut into pieces
- Olive oil baking spray
- 4 grams (1 teaspoon) baking soda
- 2 eggs, whisked lightly
- 60 grams (½ cup) walnuts, cut up
- 145 grams (1 cup) dates, pitted and cut up
- 75 grams (½ cup) raisins
- 1¼ grams (¼ teaspoon) salt
- 130 grams (1 cup) all-purpose flour
- 2 grams (½ teaspoon) baking powder
- 5 millilitres (1 teaspoon) vanilla extract

Directions:

1. In a medium-sized saucepan, put in water, dates, prunes and raisins on burner at around medium-high heat.
2. Cook the mixture until boiling.
3. Cook for around 5 minutes.
4. Blend in butter and salt and take off from burner.
5. Set the pan aside to cool thoroughly.
6. For preheating: set your oven at 175 °C (350 °F).
7. Spray a (12 cups) muffin tin with baking spray.
8. In a basin, put in flour, baking powder and baking soda and blend to incorporate.
9. In another basin, put in date mixture, eggs and vanilla extract and whisk to incorporate thoroughly.
10. Put in flour mixture and lightly blend to incorporate.
11. Lightly blend in the walnuts.
12. Place the blended mixture into muffin cups.
13. Bake in your oven for around 15-20 minutes.
14. Take off the muffin tin from oven and put onto a counter to cool for around 10 minutes.
15. Take off the muffins from tin and shift onto a platter to cool thoroughly before enjoying.

Sun-Dried Tomato Muffins

Servings | 6   Time | 30 minutes
Nutritional Content (per serving):
Cal | 453   Fat | 23.4g   Protein | 8.1g   Carbs | 58.2g   Fibre | 5.1g

Ingredients:

- ❖ 40 grams (1/3 cup) sun-dried tomatoes
- ❖ 7 grams (1¾ teaspoons) baking powder
- ❖ 2 grams (½ teaspoon) baking soda
- ❖ 1 large-sized egg
- ❖ 60 millilitres (¼ cup) olive oil
- ❖ 5 grams (3 tablespoons) fresh basil, finely cut up
- ❖ 260 grams (2 cups) white whole-wheat flour
- ❖ 2½ grams (½ teaspoon) sea salt
- ❖ 240 millilitres (1 cup) buttermilk
- ❖ 115 grams (4 ounces) soft goat cheese, crumbled

Directions:

1. For preheating: set your oven at 190 °C (375 °F).
2. Lay out paper liners in a (12 cups) muffin tin.
3. In a small-sized basin, soak the sun-dried tomatoes in hot water for around 10 minutes.
4. Drain the sun-dried tomatoes and chop them. Put it aside.
5. In a large-sized basin, put in flour, baking powder, baking soda and salt and blend to incorporate.
6. In another basin, put in egg, buttermilk and olive oil and whisk to incorporate thoroughly.
7. Make a well in the center of flour mixture.
8. Place the oil mixture into the well and with a spatula, blend to incorporate.
9. Lightly blend in the goat cheese, sun-dried tomatoes and basil.
10. Put the blended mixture into muffin cups.
11. Bake in your oven for around 12-15 minutes.
12. Take off the muffin tin from oven and place onto a counter to cool for around 9-10 minutes.
13. Take out the muffins from tin and enjoy warm.

Mixed Veggie Muffins

Servings | 8 Time | 30 minutes
Nutritional Content (per serving):
Cal | 103 Fat | 7.5g Protein | 7g Carbs | 2.7g Fibre | 0.7g

Ingredients:

- ❖ Olive oil baking spray
- ❖ 6 large-sized eggs
- ❖ 55 grams (½ cup) sun-dried tomatoes in oil, liquid removed and cut up
- ❖ 45 grams (¼ cup) canned artichokes in oil, liquid removed and thinly sliced
- ❖ 10 grams (¼ cup) fresh parsley, cut up
- ❖ 60 grams (¼ cup) half-and-half
- ❖ Salt and powdered black pepper, as desired
- ❖ 70 grams (1/3 cup) canned olives, liquid removed, pitted, and quartered
- ❖ 55 grams (¼ cup) Asiago cheese, shredded
- ❖ 30 grams (¼ cup) feta cheese, crumbled

Directions:

1. For preheating: set your oven at 190 °C (375 °F).
2. Spray 24 cups of mini muffin tins with baking spray.
3. In a basin, put in half-and-half, eggs, salt and pepper and whisk to incorporate thoroughly.
4. In a second large-sized basin, put in vegetables and Asiago cheese and blend to incorporate.
5. Place the egg mixture into muffin cups around ¾ of full.
6. Put the vegetable mixture over egg mixture and top with the remnant egg mixture.
7. Sprinkle each cup with feta and parsley.
8. Bake in your oven for around 12 minutes.
9. Take off the muffin tin from oven and place onto a counter to cool for around 4-5 minutes.
10. Take off the muffins from tin and enjoy warm.

Sun-Dried Tomato Bread

Servings|8 Time|1 hour
Nutritional Content (per serving):
Cal| 204   Fat| 3.8g   Protein| 5.8g   Carbs| 36.4g   Fibre| 1.7g

Ingredients:

- 340 grams (12 ounces) self-rising flour
- 5 grams (1 teaspoon) dried parsley
- 5 grams (1 teaspoon) dried oregano
- 240 millilitres (1 cup) milk
- 55 grams (2 ounces) sun-dried tomatoes, liquid removed and cut up

- 5 grams (1 teaspoon) white sugar
- 5 grams (1 teaspoon) dried basil
- 5 grams (1 teaspoon) dried oregano
- 20 grams (1 tablespoon) tomato puree
- 15 millilitres (1 tablespoon) olive oil

Directions:

1. For preheating: set your oven at 190 °C (375 °F).
2. Lay out a bakery paper into a loaf pan.
3. Place flour, sugar and dried herbs in a basin and blend to incorporate.
4. In a separate basin, put in milk, tomato puree and oil and whisk to incorporate thoroughly.
5. Add sundries tomatoes and blend to incorporate.
6. Put in milk mixture into the basin of flour mixture and blend to incorporate.
7. Place the bread mixture into loaf pan.
8. Bake in your oven for around 45 minutes.
9. Take off from oven and place the loaf pan onto a counter to cool for around 9-10 minutes.
10. Take off the bread from loaf pan and shift onto a platter to cool thoroughly before enjoying.

31

Olives Bread

Servings | 12   Time | 1 hour
Nutritional Content (per serving):
Cal | 164   Fat | 12.9g   Protein | 7.5g   Carbs | 7.2g   Fibre | 2.7g

Ingredients:

- 250 grams (2½ cups) almond meal
- 8 grams (2 teaspoons) baking powder
- 6 large-sized eggs
- 12 large-sized olives, pitted and cut up
- 10 grams (2 tablespoons) mixed dried herbs
- 25 grams (3 tablespoons) tapioca flour
- Pinch of salt
- 180 millilitres (¾ cup) sparkling water
- 4 cloves garlic, crushed

Directions:

1. For preheating: set your oven at 175 °C (350 °F).
2. Lay out a bakery paper into a loaf pan.
3. Place almond meal, tapioca flour, baking powder and salt in a basin and blend to incorporate.
4. In a separate basin, put in eggs and sparkling water and whisk to incorporate thoroughly.
5. Put in olives, garlic and herbs and blend to incorporate thoroughly.
6. Place the bread mixture into loaf pan.
7. Bake in your oven for around 45 minutes.
8. Take off from oven and place the loaf pan onto a counter to cool for around 9-10 minutes.
9. Take off the bread from loaf pan and shift onto a platter to cool thoroughly before enjoying.

Avocado & Eggs Toast

Servings|4   Time|20 minutes
Nutritional Content (per serving):
Cal| 197   Fat| 15.4g   Protein| 7.9g   Carbs| 8.5g   Fibre| 4g

Ingredients:

- ❖ 1 large-sized avocado, peel removed, pitted and roughly cut up
- ❖ 5 grams (2 tablespoons) fresh mint leaves, finely cut up
- ❖ 4 hard-boiled eggs, peel removed and sliced
- ❖ 1¼ millilitres (¼ teaspoon) lemon juice
- ❖ Salt and powdered black pepper, as desired
- ❖ 4 large-sized rye bread slices
- ❖ 15 grams (2 tablespoons) feta cheese, crumble

Directions:

1. In a medium-sized basin, put in avocado and with a fork, mash roughly.
2. Put in lemon juice, mint, salt and pepper and blend to incorporate thoroughly. Put it aside.
3. Heat an anti-sticking wok on burner at around medium-high heat.
4. Toast 1 bread slice for around 2 minutes from both sides.
5. Toast the remnant slices in the same method.
6. Put avocado mixture over each toasted bread slice.
7. Top with feta and enjoy immediately.

Honeyed Feta & Pear Toast

Servings | 6   Time | 20 minutes
Nutritional Content (per serving):
Cal | 220   Fat | 8.4g   Protein | 9.9g   Carbs | 26.7g   Fibre | 2.8g

Ingredients:

- ❖ 110 grams (1 cup) feta cheese
- ❖ 5 grams (2 teaspoons) orange zest, grated
- ❖ 1¼ millilitres (¼ teaspoon) almond extract
- ❖ 1 pear, halved, cored and sliced
- ❖ 50 grams (½ cup) almonds, sliced
- ❖ 20 grams (4 teaspoon) honey, divided
- ❖ 6 whole-grain bread slices, toasted
- ❖ 10 grams (1 tablespoon) almonds, sliced

Directions:

1. For the ricotta spread: in a medium-sized basin, put in feta cheese, almonds, orange zest, 5 grams of honey and almond extract and gently blend to incorporate.
2. Lay out the bread slices onto serving plates.
3. Place the ricotta mixture over each bread slice and spread in an even layer.
4. Top each slice with pear slices, followed by the almond slices.
5. Drizzle with remnant honey and enjoy immediately.

Meat Recipes

Lamb Pita Pockets

Servings | 4   Time | 10 minutes
Nutritional Content (per serving):
Cal | 385   Fat | 10.4g   Protein | 34.8g   Carbs | 39.7g   Fibre | 5.4g

Ingredients:

- ❖ 2 cloves garlic, finely cut up
- ❖ Salt and powdered black pepper, as desired
- ❖ 340 grams (¾ pound) boneless leg of lamb, cut into small pieces
- ❖ 180 grams (1½ cups) cucumber, finely cut up
- ❖ 4 (150-gram) (6-ounce) whole-wheat pita breads, warmed
- ❖ 5 grams (1 tablespoon) fresh rosemary, finely cut up
- ❖ 10 millilitres (2 teaspoons) olive oil
- ❖ 1 (150-gram) (6-ounce) container plain Greek yogurt
- ❖ 15 millilitres (1 tablespoon) lemon juice

Directions:

1. In a large-sized basin, blend all together garlic, rosemary, salt and pepper.
2. Put in lamb pieces and toss it all to mingle nicely.
3. In a large-sized, anti-sticking wok, sizzle oil on burner at around-high heat.
4. Put in lamb mixture into wok and stir fry for around 4-5 minutes.
5. Meanwhile, for yogurt sauce: in a basin, blend all together yogurt, cucumber, lemon juice, salt and pepper.
6. Lay out the lamb mixture between all the pitas.
7. Enjoy immediately with the drizzling of yogurt sauce.

Lamb Chops with Pistachios

Servings | 4   Time | 25 minutes
Nutritional Content (per serving):
Cal | 465   Fat | 21.1g   Protein | 64.2g   Carbs | 1.2g   Fibre | 0.4g

Ingredients:

- 2½ grams (½ teaspoon) ground coriander
- 1/8 teaspoon ground cinnamon
- 8 (115-gram) (4-ounce) lamb loin chops, fat removed
- 1 clove garlic, finely cut up
- 5 grams (2 teaspoons) lemon peel, grated finely
- Salt, as desired

- 2½ grams (½ teaspoon) ground cumin
- Salt and powdered black pepper, as desired
- 15 millilitres (1 tablespoon) olive oil
- 15 grams (2 tablespoons) pistachios, finely cut up
- 1½ tablespoons fresh coriander, cut up
- 1½ tablespoons fresh parsley, cut up

Directions:

1. For chops: in a large-sized basin, blend all together spices, salt and pepper.
2. Put in lamb chops and blend with spice mixture.
3. In a large-sized wok, sizzle oil on burner at around medium-high heat.
4. Sear the chops for around 4 minutes from both sides.
5. Meanwhile, for topping in a basin, blend all together remnant ingredients.
6. Enjoy the chops with the topping of pistachio mixture.

Seared Lamb Chops

Servings|4   Time|23 minutes
Nutritional Content (per serving):
Cal| 594   Fat| 35.4g   Protein| 64.2g   Carbs| 2.3g   Fibre| 0.8g

Ingredients:

- 8 bone-in lamb loin chops
- 5 grams 5 grams (1 teaspoon) powdered black pepper
- 55 grams (¼ cup) salted butter
- 5 grams (1 tablespoon) fresh rosemary, cut up

- Salt, as desired
- 30 millilitres (2 tablespoons) olive oil
- 4 cloves garlic, finely cut up
- 5 grams (1 tablespoon) fresh thyme, cut up

Directions:

1. Rub the lamb chops with salt and pepper.
2. In a large-sized cast-iron wok, sizzle the oil on burner at around medium-high heat.
3. cook the lamb chops for around 3-4 minutes from both sides.
4. Blend in butter, garlic and fresh herbs and immediately turn down the heat medium-low.
5. Cook for around 5 minutes, spooning the butter sauce over chops time to time.
6. Enjoy hot.

Leg of Lamb & Potatoes

Servings|8   Time|1½ hours
Nutritional Content (per serving):
Cal| 700   Fat| 29.9g   Protein| 68.1g   Carbs| 37.9g   Fibre| 6.5g

Ingredients:

- ❖ 1 (4-pound) bone-in leg of lamb, fat removed
- ❖ 5 whole cloves garlic, peel removed
- ❖ 10 grams (2 teaspoons) dried oregano
- ❖ 5 grams 5 grams (1 teaspoon) ground nutmeg
- ❖ 5 cloves garlic, sliced
- ❖ 1 medium-sized onion, peel removed and cut into wedges
- ❖ 5 grams (1 teaspoon) paprika
- ❖ 60 millilitres 60 millilitres (¼ cup) lemon juice
- ❖ 10 grams (2 teaspoons) dried mint
- ❖ 20 grams (4 teaspoons) paprika, divided
- ❖ Salt and powdered black pepper, as desired
- ❖ 8 medium potatoes, peel removed and cut into wedges
- ❖ 5 grams (1 teaspoon) garlic powder
- ❖ 480 millilitres (2 cups) water

Directions:

1. Take off the leg of lamb from the refrigerator and put it aside in room temperature for around 1 hour before cooking.
2. For spice mixture: in a food mixer, put in oil, lemon juice, whole garlic cloves, dried herbs, 15 grams of paprika and nutmeg and process to form a smooth mixture.
3. Shift the spice mixture into a basin and put it aside.
4. For preheating: set your oven at broiler of the oven.
5. With paper towels, pat dry the leg of lamb thoroughly.
6. With a knife, make a few slits on both sides the leg of lamb and ten rub with salt and pepper.
7. Place the leg of lamb onto a wire rack and arrange the rack onto the top oven rack.
8. Broil for around 5-7 minutes from both sides.
9. Take off from oven and shift the leg of lamb onto a platter to cool slightly.
10. Now, set your oven at 190 °C (375 °F).
11. Lay out a rack in the middle of oven.
12. Lay out a wire rack into a large-sized roasting pan.
13. Insert the garlic slices in the slits of leg of lamb and rub with spice mixture.
14. In a basin, put in potato, onion, garlic powder, remnant paprika and a little salt and toss it all to mingle nicely.
15. Put in water into the bottom of the roasting pan
16. Place the leg of lamb in the middle of the prepared roasting pan and arrange the potato and onion wedges around the lamb.
17. With a large-sized piece of heavy-duty foil, cover the roasting pan.
18. Roast in your oven for around 1 hour.
19. Take off the foil and Roast in your oven for around 10-15 minutes more.

20. Take off from oven and place the leg of lamb onto a chopping block for at least 20 minutes before carving.
21. Divide into serving-sized portions and enjoy alongside potatoes.

Lamb Shanks with Potatoes

Servings | 2   Time | 1 hour 55 minutes
Nutritional Content (per serving):
Cal | 914   Fat | 39.8g   Protein | 51.3g   Carbs | 85g   Fibre | 16.5g

Ingredients:

- ❖ 25 grams (3 tablespoons) all-purpose flour
- ❖ 30 millilitres (2 tablespoons) olive oil
- ❖ 1 (400-gram) (14-ounce) can diced tomatoes with juices
- ❖ 5 grams 5 grams (1 teaspoon) ground cinnamon
- ❖ 360 millilitres (1½ cups) water
- ❖ 5 grams (3 tablespoons) fresh parsley, cut up

- ❖ 2 lamb shanks, fat removed
- ❖ 1 medium-sized onion, cut up
- ❖ 5 grams (1 teaspoon) dried oregano
- ❖ 5 grams (1 teaspoon) dried thyme
- ❖ 2½ grams (½ teaspoon) ground allspice
- ❖ 2 potatoes, peel removed and cut up into eights
- ❖ Salt and powdered black pepper, as desired

Directions:

1. Put the flour onto a smooth counter.
2. Roll the lamb shanks in flour.
3. In a large-sized Dutch oven, sizzle the oil on burner at around medium-high heat.
4. Sear the shanks for around 5 minutes.
5. Shift the shanks onto a platter.
6. In the same Dutch oven, put in onion on burner at around medium heat.
7. Cook for around 5 minutes.
8. Put in cooked shanks, tomatoes, dried herbs, cinnamon, allspice and water and blend to incorporate.
9. Cook the shank mixture with a cover until boiling.
10. Immediately turn down the heat at around low and cook with a cover for around 25-30 minutes.
11. Take off the lid and blend in potatoes.
12. Cook with a cover for around 40-60 minutes.
13. Blend in salt, pepper and parsley and enjoy hot.

Herbed Steak

Servings | 6   Time | 20 minutes
Nutritional Content (per serving):
Cal | 301   Fat | 12.8g   Protein | 42.3g   Carbs | 1.6g   Fibre | 0.8g

Ingredients:

- ❖ Olive oil baking spray
- ❖ 3 cloves garlic, finely cut up
- ❖ 5 grams (1 tablespoon) fresh thyme, cut up
- ❖ 5 grams (1 tablespoon) fresh oregano, cut up
- ❖ 5 grams (1 tablespoon) fresh rosemary, cut up
- ❖ 955 grams (2 pounds) flank steak, fat removed
- ❖ Salt and powdered black pepper, as desired

Directions:

1. For preheating: set your grill to medium-high heat.
2. Spray the grill grate.
3. For the steak: in a large-sized basin, put in garlic and remnant ingredients except the steak and blend to incorporate thoroughly.
4. Rub the steak with blended mixture.
5. Put it aside for around 15 minutes.
6. Lay out the steak onto your grill and cook for around 12-15 minutes, changing the side after every 3-4 minutes.
7. Take off the steak from grill and shift onto a chopping block for around 5 minutes.
8. Divide the steak into serving-sized portions and enjoy.

Steak with Yogurt Sauce

Servings | 6   Time | 30 minutes
Nutritional Content (per serving):
Cal | 346   Fat | 13g   Protein | 48.9g   Carbs | 6.4g   Fibre | 1.1g

Ingredients:

- ❖ Olive oil baking spray
- ❖ 5 grams (2 tablespoons) fresh rosemary, cut up
- ❖ 375 grams (1½ cups) plain Greek yogurt
- ❖ 1 cucumber, peel removed, seeded and finely cut up
- ❖ 1¼ grams (¼ teaspoon) cayenne pepper powder
- ❖ 4 cloves garlic, finely cut up and divided
- ❖ Salt and powdered black pepper, as desired
- ❖ 955 grams (2 pounds) flank steak, fat removed
- ❖ 20 grams (1 cup) fresh parsley, cut up
- ❖ 5 grams (1 teaspoon) lemon zest, grated finely

Directions:

1. For preheating: set your grill to medium-high heat.
2. Spray the grill grate with baking spray.
3. For steak: in a large-sized basin, blend all together 3 cloves of garlic, rosemary, salt and pepper.
4. Rub the steak with garlic mixture.
5. Set it aside for around 15 minutes.
6. Lay down the steak onto your grill and cook for around 12-15 minutes, turning the side after every 3-4 minutes.
7. Shift the steak onto chopping block and put it aside for around 5 minutes.
8. Meanwhile, for sauce: in a basin, blend all together 1 clove of garlic and remnant ingredients.
9. Divide the steak into serving-sized portions and enjoy with a topping of yogurt sauce.

Beef & Veggie Stew

Servings│6   Time│1 hour 5 minutes
Nutritional Content (per serving):
Cal│ 388   Fat│ 17.7g   Protein│ 48.5g   Carbs│ 8g   Fibre│ 3.1g

Ingredients:

- 30 millilitres (2 tablespoons) olive oil
- 2 cloves garlic, cut up
- 1 (400-gram) (14-ounce) can crushed tomatoes
- 5 grams (1 teaspoon) red pepper flakes
- 225 grams (8 ounces) fresh baby spinach
- Salt and powdered black pepper, as needed

- 1 small-sized onion, cut up
- 955 grams (2 pounds) beef chuck, cut into cubes
- 10 grams (2 teaspoons) ground allspice
- 120 millilitres (½ cup) beef broth
- 30 millilitres (2 tablespoons) lemon juice
- 5 grams (¼ cup) fresh parsley, cut up

Directions:

1. In a large-sized saucepan, sizzle the oil in a saucepan on burner at around high heat.
2. Cook the onion and garlic for around 2-3 minutes.
3. Put in beef and cook for around 3-4 minutes, mixing all the time.
4. Put in tomatoes, spices and broth.
5. Cook the mixture until boiling.
6. Immediately turn down the heat at around low.
7. Cook with a cover for around 30-40 minutes.
8. Blend in olives and spinach and cook for around 2-3 minutes.
9. Blend in lemon juice, salt and pepper and take off from burner.
10. Enjoy hot with the decoration of parsley.

Tomato-Braised Beef

Servings | 8   Time | 2 hours 10 minutes
Nutritional Content (per serving):
Cal | 453   Fat | 17.9g   Protein | 53.9g   Carbs | 12.1g   Fibre | 3.3g

Ingredients:

- ❖ 60 millilitres (¼ cup) olive oil
- ❖ 3 celery stalks, cut up
- ❖ 2 onions, cut up
- ❖ 2 (800-gram) (28-ounce) cans stewed tomatoes
- ❖ 5 grams (1 teaspoon) dried oregano
- ❖ 1365 grams (3 pounds) boneless beef chuck roast, cut into cubes
- ❖ 4 cloves garlic, finely cut up
- ❖ 240 millilitres (1 cup) dry red wine
- ❖ 10 grams (½ cup) fresh parsley, cut up
- ❖ Salt and powdered black pepper, as desired

Directions:

1. In a large-sized saucepan, sizzle the oil on burner at around medium-high heat.
2. Sear the beef cubes for around 4-5 minutes.
3. Put in celery, onions and garlic and cook for around 5 minutes, mixing all the time.
4. Blend in the remnant ingredients.
5. Cook the mixture until boiling.
6. Immediately turn down the heat at around low.
7. Cook with a cover for around 1½-1¾ hours.
8. Enjoy hot.

Beef Gyro

Servings | 10   Time | 1¼ hours
Nutritional Content (per serving):
Cal | 179   Fat | 6g   Protein | 27.9g   Carbs | 2.1g   Fibre | 0.8g

Ingredients:

- ½ onion, finely cut up
- 3 cloves garlic, finely cut up
- 5 grams (1 teaspoon) dried rosemary
- 5 grams (1 teaspoon) dried thyme
- 5 grams (paprika)
- 1¼ grams (¼ teaspoon) sea salt

- 955 grams (2 pounds) ground beef
- 5 grams (1 teaspoon) dried oregano
- 5 grams (1 teaspoon) dried mint
- 5 grams (1 teaspoon) ground cumin
- 5 grams (1 teaspoon) powdered black pepper

Directions:

1. Put the cut up onion onto the center of a kitchen towel.
2. Gather up the ends of towel and squeeze tightly to remove liquid.
3. In a large-sized basin, put in onion and remnant ingredients and blend to incorporate thoroughly.
4. Cover the basin of lamb mixture and shift into your refrigerator for around 1-2 hours.
5. For preheating: set your oven at 165 °C (325 °F).
6. Lay out a damp kitchen towel into a large-sized roasting pan.
7. In a food mixer, put in lamb mixture and process for around 1 minute.
8. Put the lamb mixture into a loaf pan and press down tightly
9. Lay out the loaf pan in the roasting pan.
10. Carefully pour boiling water into the roasting pan around halfway up the sides of loaf pan.
11. Bake in your oven for around 45-60 minutes.
12. Take off the loaf pan from oven and discard the any accumulated grease.
13. Lay down the loaf pan onto a counter to cool slightly before enjoying.

Beef Bifteki

Servings | 4   Time | 35 minutes
Nutritional Content (per serving):
Cal | 369   Fat | 15.8g   Protein | 51.6g   Carbs | 1.8g   Fibre | 0.2g

Ingredients:

- ❖ Olive oil baking spray
- ❖ 650 grams (1 1/3 pounds) ground beef
- ❖ 10 grams (2 teaspoons) dried thyme
- ❖ Salt and powdered black pepper, as desired
- ❖ 15 grams (1 tablespoon) plain Greek yogurt
- ❖ 115 grams (4 ounces) feta cheese, cut into 4 slices

Directions:

1. For preheating your grill for indirect heat.
2. Spray the grill grate.
3. In a large-sized basin, put in ground beef, yogurt, thyme, salt and pepper and blend to incorporate thoroughly.
4. Shape the blended beef mixture into eight patties.
5. Place 1 cheese slice between two patties, and press slightly to seal the edges.
6. Repeat with remnant beef patties and cheese slices.
7. Place he patties onto your grill and cover it.
8. Cook for around 15-20 minutes.
9. Enjoy hot.

Pork Chops with Peaches

Servings | 4   Time | 35 minutes
Nutritional Content (per serving):
Cal | 477   Fat | 30.3g   Protein | 39g   Carbs | 14.5g   Fibre | 1.7g

Ingredients:

- 4 bone-in pork chops
- 30 millilitres (2 tablespoons) extra-virgin olive oil
- 5 grams (1 tablespoon) fresh oregano, cut up
- 10 grams (½ cup) fresh basil, cut up
- Salt and powdered black pepper, as needed
- 120 millilitres (½ cup) balsamic vinegar
- 20 grams (1 tablespoon) honey
- 2 peaches, pitted and sliced
- 150 grams (6 ounces) feta cheese, crumbled
- 1¼ grams (¼ teaspoon) red pepper flakes

Directions:

1. For preheating: set your oven at broiler of the oven.
2. Rub the pork chops with the salt and pepper.
3. In a large-sized ovenproof wok, sizzle the oil on burner at around medium-high heat.
4. Sear the pork chops for around 3-4 minutes from both sides.
5. Immediately turn down the heat at around medium.
6. Cook for around 6-8 minutes.
7. In a small-sized basin, put in vinegar, honey and oregano and whisk to blend thoroughly.
8. Blend in vinegar mixture and cook for around 2 minutes.
9. Take off from burner and blend in peaches.
10. Shift the wok to the oven and broil for around 4-5 minutes.
11. Take off from oven and enjoy hot with the topping of feta, basil and red pepper flakes.

Pork & Veggies Bake

Servings|8   Time|1 hour
Nutritional Content (per serving):
Cal| 569   Fat| 21.2g   Protein| 55.1g   Carbs| 38.1g   Fibre| 6.8g

Ingredients:

- 5 grams (1 teaspoon) dried thyme
- 5 grams (1 teaspoon) ground coriander
- 2 (680-gram) (1½-pound) pork tenderloins, halved crosswise
- 1 large-sized fennel bulb, trimmed and cut into small chunks
- 2 jalapeño peppers, halved lengthwise, seeded and sliced
- 5 grams (1 teaspoon) granulated garlic
- Salt and powdered black pepper, as needed
- 60 millilitres (¼ cup) olive oil, divided
- 10 small-sized white potatoes, cut into small chunks
- 1 large-sized onion, cut into small chunks
- 10 fresh thyme sprigs

Directions:

1. For preheating: set your oven at 220 °C (425 °F).
2. In a small-sized basin, blend all together the thyme, garlic, coriander, salt and pepper.
3. Rub the pork tenderloins with spice mixture.
4. In a large-sized heavy-bottomed wok, sizzle 30 millilitres (2 tablespoons) of oil on burner at around high heat.
5. Sear the pork loins for around 6 minutes.
6. Take off from burner and put it aside.
7. In a large-sized rimmed baking tray, put in potatoes, fennel, onions, jalapeños, remnant oil and salt and pepper and toss it all to mingle nicely.
8. Lay out the thyme sprigs on top and tuck the thyme leaves amongst the vegetables.
9. Lay down the pork pieces on top and gently push into the vegetables.
10. Roast in your oven for around 30 minutes.
11. Take off from oven a shift the pork pieces onto a chopping block.
12. With a piece of heavy-duty foil, cover the pork pieces lightly.
13. Roast the vegetables in your oven for around 10 minutes more.
14. Cut each pork piece into serving-sized portions and enjoy with roasted vegetables.

Pistachio Pork Tenderloin

Servings | 4   Time | 35 minutes
Nutritional Content (per serving):
Cal | 258   Fat | 9.8g   Protein | 30.8g   Carbs | 11.8g   Fibre | 0.6g

Ingredients:

- 50 grams (1/3 cup) pistachios, shelled and toasted
- Salt and powdered black pepper, as desired
- 15 millilitres (1 tablespoon) extra-virgin olive oil
- 2 cloves garlic, peel removed
- 455 grams (1 pound) pork tenderloin, fat removed
- 35 grams (3 tablespoons) orange marmalade

Directions:

1. Lay out a rack in the center of oven.
2. For preheating: set your oven at 230 °C (450 °F).
3. In a mini food mixer, put in pistachios and garlic and process until finely cut up.
4. Rub the pork tenderloin with salt and pepper.
5. In a large-sized cast-iron wok, sizzle the oil on burner at around medium-high heat.
6. Cook the pork for around 4-6 minutes.
7. Take off the wok from burner.
8. Coat the top of pork with orange marmalade, followed by pistachio mixture.
9. With your hands, lightly press the pistachio mixture into the meat.
10. Roast in your oven for around 12-16 minutes.
11. Take off from oven and shift the pork tenderloin onto a chopping block for around 4-5 minutes.
12. Cut the pork tenderloin into serving-sized portions and enjoy.

Pork Souvlaki

Servings | 5   Time | 25 minutes
Nutritional Content (per serving):
Cal | 292   Fat | 15.1g   Protein | 36g   Carbs | 1.9g   Fibre | 0.7g

Ingredients:

- ❖ 60 millilitres 60 millilitres (¼ cup) extra-virgin olive oil
- ❖ 30 millilitres (2 tablespoons) red wine vinegar
- ❖ 5 grams (1 tablespoon) fresh oregano, cut up
- ❖ Salt and powdered black pepper, as desired

- ❖ 45 millilitres (3 tablespoons) lemon juice
- ❖ 3 cloves garlic, finely cut up
- ❖ 5 grams (1 tablespoon) fresh thyme, cut up
- ❖ 5 grams (1 teaspoon) lemon zest, grated
- ❖ 680 grams (1½ pounds) pork tenderloin, cut into cubes

Directions:

1. In a large-sized basin, put in   and remnant ingredients except for pork cubes and blend to incorporate thoroughly.
2. Put in pork cubes and blend with the blended mixture.
3. Cover the basin and shift into your refrigerator to marinate for all the night.
4. For preheating: set your outdoor grill to medium-high heat. Spray the grill grate.
5. Thread the pork cubes onto the pre-soaked bamboo skewers
6. Place the skewers onto your grill and cook for around 10-12 minutes, changing the side after every 2-3 minutes.
7. Enjoy immediately.

Poultry Recipes

Lemony Chicken Breasts

Servings│4   Time│22 minutes
Nutritional Content (per serving):
Cal│ 315   Fat│ 19.1g   Protein│ 33.2g   Carbs│ 1.6g   Fibre│ 0.5g

Ingredients:

- ❖ 4 (115-gram) (4-ounce) boneless chicken breast halves
- ❖ 45 millilitres (3 tablespoons) olive oil
- ❖ 5 grams (1 teaspoon) paprika
- ❖ 2½ grams (½ teaspoon) dried oregano
- ❖ Olive oil baking spray
- ❖ 3 cloves garlic, finely cut up
- ❖ 5 grams (3 tablespoons) fresh parsley, cut up
- ❖ 45 millilitres (3 tablespoons) lemon juice
- ❖ Salt and powdered black pepper, as desired

Directions:

1. With a fork, pierce chicken breasts several times
2. In a large-sized basin, put in garlic and remnant ingredients except the chicken breasts and blend to incorporate thoroughly.
3. Put in chicken breasts and blend with the marinade.
4. Shift into your refrigerator to marinate for around 2-3 hours.
5. For preheating: set your grill to medium-high heat.
6. Spray the grill grate with baking spray.
7. Lay down the chicken breasts onto the grill.
8. Cook for around 5-6 minutes from both sides.
9. Enjoy hot.

Dill-Braised Chicken

Servings | 6   Time | 1¼ hours
Nutritional Content (per serving):
Cal | 514   Fat | 22.5g   Protein | 69.2g   Carbs | 4.6g   Fibre | 0.5g

Ingredients:

- ❖ 6 (225-gram) (8-ounce) bone-in chicken thighs
- ❖ ½ of onion, sliced
- ❖ 2½ grams (½ teaspoon) ground turmeric
- ❖ 30 millilitres (2 tablespoons) lemon juice
- ❖ 15 millilitres (1 tablespoon) water
- ❖ Salt and powdered black pepper, as desired

- ❖ 30 millilitres (2 tablespoons) olive oil
- ❖ 960 millilitres (4 cups) chicken broth
- ❖ 8 fresh dill sprigs
- ❖ 15 grams (2 tablespoons) arrowroot starch
- ❖ 5 grams (1 tablespoon) fresh dill, cut up

Directions:

1. Rub the chicken thighs with salt and pepper.
2. In a large-sized anti-sticking wok, sizzle the oil on burner at around high heat.
3. Lay down the chicken thighs in wok, skin side down.
4. Cook for around 3-4 minutes.
5. With a frying ladle, shift the thighs onto a plate.
6. In the same wok, put in onion on burner at around medium heat.
7. Cook for around 4-5 minutes.
8. Lay out the thighs in wok, skin side up with broth, turmeric, salt and pepper.
9. Place the dill sprigs and over thighs.
10. Cook the mixture until boiling.
11. Immediately turn down the heat medium-low.
12. Cook with a cover for around 40-45 minutes, coating the thighs with cooking liquid time to time.
13. Meanwhile, in a small-sized basin, blend all together arrowroot starch and water.
14. Discard the thyme sprigs and shift the thighs into a basin.
15. Put in lemon juice in sauce and blend to incorporate.
16. Slowly, put in arrowroot starch mixture, mixing all the time.
17. Cook for around 3-4 minutes, mixing time to time.
18. Enjoy hot with the declaration of cut up dill.

Dried Fruit-Braised Chicken Legs

Servings | 8   Time | 1 hour
Nutritional Content (per serving):
Cal | 513   Fat | 33.9g   Protein | 40.8g   Carbs | 15.4g   Fibre | 3.1g

Ingredients:

- ❖ 2½ grams (½ teaspoon) paprika
- ❖ 1¼ grams (¼ teaspoon) ground cumin
- ❖ 8 bone-in chicken leg quarters
- ❖ 1 onion, sliced
- ❖ 2 cloves garlic, finely cut up
- ❖ 20 grams (1 tablespoon) tomato paste
- ❖ 85 grams (½ cup) dried apricots, pitted
- ❖ 60 millilitres (¼ cup) orange juice
- ❖ 1 bay leaf
- ❖ 1¼ grams (¼ teaspoon) ground cinnamon
- ❖ Salt and powdered black pepper, as desired
- ❖ 45 millilitres (3 tablespoons) olive oil, divided
- ❖ 6 ripe plum tomatoes, cut up
- ❖ 180 grams (1 cup) green olives, pitted
- ❖ 240 millilitres (1 cup) chicken broth
- ❖ 5 grams (3 tablespoons) fresh parsley, cut up

Directions:

1. In a small-sized basin, blend all together the spices, salt and pepper.
2. Rub the chicken legs with spice mixture.
3. In a deep, heavy-bottomed wok, sizzle 30 millilitres (2 tablespoons) of oil on burner at around medium-high heat.
4. Cook the chicken legs for around 3-5 minutes from both sides.
5. With a frying ladle, shift the chicken legs onto a platter.
6. In the same wok, sizzle the remnant oil on burner at around medium heat.
7. Cook the onion and garlic for around 2 minutes.
8. Blend in tomatoes, tomato paste, olives, apricots, prunes, broth, orange juice and bay leaf.
9. Cook the mixture until boiling..
10. Put in cooked chicken and blend to incorporate.
11. Immediately turn down the heat low.
12. Cook with a cover for around 30 minutes.
13. Enjoy hot with the decoration of parsley.

Chicken & Carrot Bake

Servings | 4   Time | 40 minutes
Nutritional Content (per serving):
Cal | 429   Fat | 21.5g . Protein | 35.3g   Carbs | 25.2g   Fibre | 5.6g

Ingredients:

- Olive oil baking spray
- 455 grams (1 pound) carrots, peel removed and cut into chunks
- 2 Medjool dates, pitted and finely cut up
- 3 green onions, sliced
- 1 (5-centimetre) (2-inch) piece fresh ginger, grated
- 10 grams (2 teaspoons) ground cumin
- 5 grams (1 teaspoon) red pepper flakes
- 10 grams (½ cup) fresh parsley, cut up
- 4 (115-gram) (4-ounce) boneless chicken thighs
- 1 navel orange, cut into 2-inch wedges
- ½ of onion, sliced thinly
- 2 cloves garlic, sliced
- 60 millilitres (¼ cup) extra-virgin olive oil
- 10 grams (2 teaspoons) dried thyme
- 10 grams (2 teaspoons) ground coriander
- Salt, as desired

Directions:

1. For preheating: set your oven at 230 °C (450 °F).
2. Spray a large-sized rimmed baking tray with baking spray.
3. In a large-sized basin, put in   and remnant ingredients except for parsley and blend to incorporate.
4. Lay out the chicken mixture onto the baking tray.
5. Roast in your oven for around 22-25 minutes.
6. Take off from oven and squeeze the orange wedges over the chicken mixture.
7. Enjoy hot with the decoration of parsley.

Stuffed Chicken Breast Rolls

Servings | 4   Time | 40 minutes
Nutritional Content (per serving):
Cal | 211   Fat | 10.5g   Protein | 27g   Carbs | 1.9g   Fibre | 0.6g

Ingredients:

- Olive oil baking spray
- Salt and powdered black pepper, as desired
- 45 grams (¼ cup) Kalamata olives, pitted and cut up
- 30 grams (¼ cup) feta cheese, crumbled
- 15 millilitres (1 tablespoon) extra-virgin olive oil
- 4 (115-gram) (4-ounce) boneless chicken breast halves, pounded slightly
- 30 grams (¼ cup) oil-packed sun-dried tomatoes, liquid removed
- 5 grams (1 tablespoon) fresh dill, cut up
- 5 grams (1 tablespoon) fresh parsley, cut up

Directions:

1. For preheating: set your oven at 190 ºC (375 ºF).
2. Spray a rimmed baking tray with baking spray.
3. Rub the chicken with salt and pepper.
4. In a large-sized basin, blend all together olives, tomatoes, feta cheese, green onion, dill, and parsley.
5. Place chicken breast onto a chopping block.
6. Place the olives mixture over chicken breast and tightly roll up.
7. Secure each breast roll with toothpicks.
8. In a wok, sizzle oil on burner at around medium heat.
9. Cook breast rolls for around 2 minutes from both sides.
10. Take off from burner and arrange the chicken rolls onto the baking tray.
11. Bake in your oven for around 16-20 minutes.
12. Take off the baking tray from oven and put it aside for around 5 minutes.
13. Divide into serving-sized portions and enjoy.

Apricot-Glazed Chicken

Servings | 4   Time | 45 minutes
Nutritional Content (per serving):
Cal | 495   Fat | 15.1g   Protein | 39g   Carbs | 47.4g   Fibre | 1.1g

Ingredients:

- 90 grams (½ cup) canned olives, liquid removed and sliced
- 5 cloves garlic, finely cut up
- 85 grams (½ cup) brown sugar
- 120 millilitres (½ cup) white wine
- 15 millilitres (1 tablespoon) caper brine
- 4 (150-gram) (6-ounce) boneless chicken breasts
- 45 grams (1/3 cup) capers, liquid removed
- 5 grams (2-(3 tablespoons) fresh coriander, cut up
- 150 grams (½ cup) apricot jam
- 90 millilitres (1/3 cup) red wine vinegar
- 30 millilitres (2 tablespoons) extra-virgin olive oil

Directions:

1. For preheating: set your oven at 175 ℃ (350 °F).
2. In a large-sized basin, put in olives and remnant ingredients except for oil and chicken breasts and blend to incorporate thoroughly. Put it aside.
3. In a large-sized wok, sizzle the oil on burner at around medium-high heat.
4. Sear the chicken breasts for around 1½ minutes from both sides.
5. Take off from burner and lay out the chicken into a baking pan.
6. Place the jam mixture on top of chicken breasts.
7. Bake in your oven for around 20-30 minutes.
8. Enjoy hot.

Chicken & Olives Bake

Servings|4 Time|1 hour
Nutritional Content (per serving):
Cal| 569   Fat| 33.4g   Protein| 49.4g   Carbs| 18.5g   Fibre| 4.9g

Ingredients:

- ❖ 115 grams (4 ounces) black olives, pitted
- ❖ 2 cloves garlic, crushed
- ❖ Salt and powdered black pepper, as needed
- ❖ 1 bay leaf
- ❖ 60 millilitres (¼ cup) olive oil
- ❖ 25 grams (2 tablespoons) sugar
- ❖ 180 millilitres (¾ cup) chicken broth

- ❖ 115 grams (4 ounces) capers
- ❖ 5 grams (2 tablespoons) fresh oregano, finely cut up
- ❖ 60 millilitres (¼ cup) balsamic vinegar
- ❖ 4 (150-gram) (6-ounce) chicken drumsticks

Directions:

1. For the marinade: in a large-sized baking pan, put in olives, capers, garlic, oregano, salt, black pepper, bay leaf, vinegar and oil and blend to incorporate thoroughly.
2. Put in chicken drumsticks and blend with the marinade.
3. Cover the baking pan and shift into your refrigerator for all the night.
4. Take off from refrigerator and put it aside for at least 1 hour before cooking.
5. For preheating: set your oven at 165 °C (325 °F).
6. Lay out the chicken drumsticks into a baking pan.
7. Spread the marinade over the chicken drumsticks.
8. Put the broth around the chicken breasts.
9. Bake in your oven for around 50 minutes.
10. Enjoy hot.

Pomegranate-Braised Chicken Thighs

Servings | 6   Time | 1 hour 20 minutes
Nutritional Content (per serving):
Cal | 467   Fat | 18.5g   Protein | 52.3g   Carbs | 17.2g   Fibre | 2.1g

Ingredients:

- 15 millilitres (1 tablespoon) white vinegar
- 6 cloves garlic, cut up
- 15 grams (1 tablespoon) seasoning salt
- 5 grams (1 teaspoon) paprika
- Powdered black pepper, as desired
- 1 large-sized onion, sliced and divided
- 120 millilitres (½ cup) dry white wine
- 600 millilitres (2½ cups) chicken broth
- 20 grams (4-5 teaspoons) dried mint
- 60 grams (1 tablespoon) pomegranate molasses, divided
- 5 grams (1 teaspoon) ground cloves
- 5 grams (1 teaspoon) ground nutmeg
- 6 (115-gram) (4-ounce) chicken thighs
- 30 millilitres (2 tablespoons) extra-virgin olive oil, divided
- 1 bay leaf
- 65 grams (1/3 cup) pomegranate seeds

Directions:

1. In a large-sized basin, put in vinegar, 20 grams of molasses, garlic and spices and blend to incorporate.
2. Put in chicken thighs and blend with the mixture.
3. In a large-sized baking pan, slay out half of the onion slices.
4. Arrange the chicken over onion slices in a single layer and shift into your refrigerator, covered for 2 hours.
5. Take off the baking pan from oven and put it aside for around 15-20 minutes before cooking.
6. For preheating: set your oven at 230 °C (450 °F).
7. In a large-sized, heavy-bottomed wok, sizzle 15 millilitres of oil on burner at around medium-high heat.
8. Cook the chicken thighs for around 2-3 minutes from both sides.
9. Take off from burner and place the chicken thighs in a large-sized roasting pan.
10. In the same wok, sizzle the remnant oil on burner at around medium-high heat.
11. Cook the remnant onion slices for around 3-5 minutes.
12. Blend in wine and cook for around 2-3 minutes.
13. Put in remnant pomegranate molasses, bay leaf, some seasoned salt and broth and blend to incorporate.
14. Immediately turn down the heat at around medium-low and cook for around 5-7 minutes.
15. Discard the bay leaf and place the sauce over the chicken thighs in the roasting pan.
16. Cover the roasting pan and bake in your oven for around 20 minutes.
17. Take off the cover and put on the lowest rack of oven.
18. Bake in your oven for around 26-30 minutes.
19. Take off from oven and put it aside for around 5 minutes before enjoying.
20. Dust with dried mint and enjoy with the decoration of pomegranate seeds.

Chicken with Artichoke Salsa

Servings | 4   Time | 25 minutes
Nutritional Content (per serving):
Cal | 453   Fat | 19.3g   Protein | 35.2g   Carbs | 8.8g   Fibre | 2.7g

Ingredients:

- ❖ 455 grams (1 pound) boneless chicken breasts, cut into thin slices
- ❖ 30 millilitres (2 tablespoons) balsamic vinegar, divided
- ❖ Olive oil baking spray
- ❖ 15 grams (2 tablespoons) sun-dried tomatoes, cut up
- ❖ 45 grams (¼ cup) Kalamata olives, pitted and cut up
- ❖ 35 grams (¼ cup) roasted red peppers, cut up
- ❖ 15 millilitres (1 tablespoon) balsamic vinegar
- ❖ 45 millilitres (3 tablespoons) olive oil, divided
- ❖ 2½ grams (½ teaspoon) garlic powder
- ❖ Salt and powdered black pepper, as desired
- ❖ 1 (400-gram) (14-ounce) can artichoke hearts, liquid removed and cut up
- ❖ 15 grams (2 tablespoons) capers, liquid removed
- ❖ 45 grams (¼ cup) green olives, pitted and cut up
- ❖ 5 grams (¼ cup) fresh parsley, cut up
- ❖ 30 millilitres (2 tablespoons) olive oil
- ❖ 30 grams (¼ cup) feta cheese, crumbled

Directions:

1. For chicken: in a large-sized glass basin, put in chicken slices, 15 millilitres of oil, 15 millilitres of vinegar, garlic powder, salt and peer and blend to incorporate.
2. Cover the basin of chicken and shift into your refrigerator to marinate for all the night.
3. Lightly spray an anti-sticking wok with baking spray and sizzle on burner at around medium-high heat.
4. Cook the chicken slices for around 6-8 minutes.
5. Meanwhile, for the salsa: in a basin, put in remnant oil and vinegar.
6. Put in remnant ingredients and blend to incorporate.
7. Take off the wok from burner and divide the chicken slices onto serving plates.
8. Enjoy immediately alongside the salsa.

Chicken & Potato Bake

Servings | 8   Time | 1 hour 25 minutes
Nutritional Content (per serving):
Cal | 611   Fat | 27.6g   Protein | 54.1g   Carbs | 35.9g   Fibre | 5.9g

Ingredients:

- 8 medium-sized Yukon Gold potatoes, scrubbed and cut each into 8 wedges
- 120 millilitres (½ cup) olive oil
- 6 cloves garlic, finely cut up
- 10 grams (2 teaspoons) salt
- 360 millilitres (1½ cups) chicken broth
- 180 grams (1 cup) Greek olives, pitted
- 8 bone-in chicken thighs
- 45 millilitres (3 tablespoons) lemon juice
- 5 grams (1 teaspoons) dried oregano
- 2½ grams (½ teaspoon) powdered black pepper

Directions:

1. For preheating: set your oven at 190 °C (375 °F).
2. In a shallow roasting pan, lay out the potato wedges and top with olives, followed by chicken thighs.
3. In a small-sized basin, put in oil, lemon juice, garlic, oregano, salt and pepper and whisk to incorporate.
4. Spread the oil mixture over chicken and potatoes.
5. Put in chicken broth around chicken and potatoes.
6. Bake in your oven for around 60-70 minutes.
7. Enjoy hot.

Chicken in Fig Sauce

Servings | 4   Time | 55 minutes
Nutritional Content (per serving):
Cal | 411   Fat | 12.7g   Protein | 51.2g   Carbs | 22.1g   Fibre | 3.3g

Ingredients:

- 4 (150-gram) (6-ounce) boneless chicken breast halves
- 2½ grams (½ teaspoon) salt, divided
- 30 millilitres (2 tablespoons) olive oil, divided
- 75 grams (½ cup) dried figs, finely cut up
- 60 millilitres (¼ cup) balsamic vinegar
- 15 grams (1 tablespoon) sugar

- 5 grams (2 tablespoons) fresh thyme, cut up and divided
- 1¼ grams (¼ teaspoon) powdered black pepper
- 90 grams (¾ cup) onion, cut up
- 120 millilitres (½ cup) chicken broth
- 10 millilitres (2 teaspoons) soy sauce

Directions:

1. In a small-sized basin, put in half of thyme, 1¼ grams of salt and pepper and blend to incorporate.
2. Rub the chicken breast halves with the thyme mixture.
3. In a large-sized cast-iron wok, sizzle 15 millilitres of oil on burner at around medium-high heat.
4. In the wok, put in chicken breasts, skin side down and cook for around 5-6 minutes from both sides.
5. With a frying ladle, shift the cooked chicken breasts onto a plate.
6. With a piece of heavy-duty foil, cover them to keep warm.
7. Sizzle the remnant oil in the same wok on burner at around medium heat.
8. Cook the onion for around 3 minutes.
9. Blend in figs, broth, vinegar, soy sauce and sugar and cook for around 3 minutes.
10. Blend in remnant thyme and salt and take off from burner.
11. Cut the chicken breast halves into slices diagonally.
12. Enjoy the chicken with the topping of fig sauce.

Chicken & Artichoke Casserole

Servings | 8   Time | 55 minutes
Nutritional Content (per serving):
Cal | 479   Fat | 22.2g   Protein | 59.6g   Carbs | 9.6g   Fibre | 3.8g

Ingredients:

- Olive oil baking spray
- Salt and powdered black pepper, as desired
- 30 millilitres (2 tablespoons) olive oil
- 1 (70-gram) (2½-ounce) can sliced black olives, liquid removed
- 1 (425-gram) (15-ounce) can tomato sauce
- 8 (150-gram) (6-ounce) boneless chicken thighs
- 1 (400-gram) (14-ounce) can quartered artichoke hearts, liquid removed
- 220 grams (2 cups) Kefalograviera cheese, shredded

Directions:

1. For preheating: set your oven at 190 ºC (375 ºF).
2. Rub the chicken thighs with the salt and pepper.
3. In a large-sized wok, sizzle the oil on burner at around medium heat.
4. Cook the chicken thighs for around 2-3 minutes from both sides.
5. Take off from burner and arrange the chicken thighs into a casserole pan.
6. Top with the artichoke hearts, followed by the olives, tomato sauce and cheese.
7. Bake in your oven for around 25-30 minutes.
8. Now, set your oven to broiler.
9. Broil for around 2-3 minutes.
10. Enjoy hot.

Chicken Souvlaki

Servings | 8   Time | 30 minutes
Nutritional Content (per serving):
Cal | 375   Fat | 18.1g   Protein | 49.5g   Carbs | 1.3g   Fibre | 0.7g

Ingredients:

- ❖ 60 millilitres (¼ cup) lemon juice
- ❖ 5 grams (2 tablespoons) fresh oregano, cut up
- ❖ 5 grams (2 teaspoons) lemon zest, grated
- ❖ 1365 grams (3 pounds) boneless chicken breasts, cubed
- ❖ 45 millilitres (3 tablespoons) olive oil
- ❖ 5 grams (1 tablespoon) fresh thyme, cut up
- ❖ 1 clove garlic, grated
- ❖ Salt and powdered black pepper, as desired
- ❖ Olive oil baking spray

Directions:

1. In a large-sized basin, put in lemon juice and remnant ingredients except for chicken cubes and blend to incorporate.
2. Put in chicken cubes and blend with marinade.
3. Cover the basin and shift into your refrigerator to marinate for at least 30 minutes.
4. For preheating: set your grill to medium-high heat.
5. Spray the grill grate with baking spray.
6. Thread the chicken cubes onto pre-soaked wooden skewers.
7. Lay down the skewers onto your grill and cook for around 5-6 minutes from both sides.
8. Enjoy hot.

Chicken & Grapes Kabobs

Servings|4 Time|25 minutes
Nutritional Content (per serving):
Cal| 311   Fat| 20.1g   Protein| 24.6g   Carbs| 9g   Fibre| 1.3g

Ingredients:

- 90 millilitres (1/3 cup) extra-virgin olive oil, divided
- 5 grams (1 tablespoon) fresh oregano, finely cut up
- 2½ grams (½ teaspoon) red chili flakes
- Olive oil baking spray
- 65 grams (1¾ cups) green seedless grapes, rinsed
- 2 cloves garlic, finely cut up
- 5 grams (1 tablespoon) fresh rosemary, finely cut up
- 5 grams (1 teaspoon) lemon zest, grated
- 455 grams (1 pound) boneless chicken breast, cut into cubes
- 2½ grams (½ teaspoon) salt
- 15 millilitres (1 tablespoon) lemon juice

Directions:

1. In a small-sized basin, put in 60 millilitres of oil, garlic, fresh herbs, lemon zest and chili flakes and whisk to incorporate thoroughly.
2. Thread the chicken cubes and grapes onto 12 metal skewers.
3. In a large-sized baking pan, arrange the skewers.
4. Place the marinade and blend to incorporate.
5. Shift into your refrigerator to marinate for around 4-24 hours.
6. For preheating: set your grill to medium-high heat.
7. Spray the grill grate with baking spray.
8. Take off the skewers from baking pan and shake off the excess marinade.
9. Now, sprinkle the skewers with salt.
10. Lay out the skewers onto your grill.
11. Cook for around 3-5 minutes from both sides.
12. Take off from grill and shift the skewers onto a serving platter.
13. Drizzle with lemon juice and remnant oil and enjoy

Chicken & Veggie Kabobs

Servings|8   Time|30 minutes
Nutritional Content (per serving):
Cal| 214   Fat| 11.2g   Protein| 29.4g   Carbs| 15.7g   Fibre| 4.7g

Ingredients:

- ❖ 60 millilitres (¼ cup) white vinegar
- ❖ 60 millilitres (¼ cup) olive oil
- ❖ 2½ grams (½ teaspoon) dried thyme
- ❖ 5 grams (1 teaspoon) ground cumin
- ❖ 955 grams (2 pounds) boneless chicken breast, cut into cubes
- ❖ 1 large-sized onion, quartered and separated into pieces
- ❖ 60 millilitres (¼ cup) lemon juice
- ❖ 2 cloves garlic, finely cut up
- ❖ 2½ grams (½ teaspoon) dried oregano
- ❖ Salt and powdered black pepper, as desired
- ❖ Olive oil baking spray
- ❖ 2 large-sized capsicums, seeded and cut into cubes
- ❖ 16 cherry tomatoes

Directions:

1. In a large-sized basin, blend all together vinegar, lemon juice oil, garlic, dried herbs, cumin, salt and pepper.
2. Put in chicken cubes and blend with mixture.
3. Cover the basin of chicken and shift into your refrigerator to marinate for around 2-4 hours.
4. For preheating: set your outdoor grill to medium-high heat.
5. Spray the grill grate with cooking spray.
6. Take off the chicken from refrigerator and discard the excess marinade.
7. Thread the chicken and vegetables onto pre-soaked wooden skewers.
8. Lay out the skewers onto your grill and cook for around 10 minutes, changing the side time to time.
9. Enjoy hot.

Seafood Recipes

Sardines with Olives

Servings | 4   Time | 23 minutes
Nutritional Content (per serving):
Cal | 301   Fat | 19.1g   Protein | 28.9g   Carbs | 3.1g   Fibre | 1.6g

Ingredients:

- ❖ 12 (55-gram) (2-ounce) fresh sardines, cleaned and scaled
- ❖ 90 grams (½ cup) green olives, pitted and cut up
- ❖ 5 grams (1 tablespoon) fresh oregano, cut up
- ❖ 2 cloves garlic, thinly sliced
- ❖ 5 grams (1 teaspoon) lemon zest, grated finely
- ❖ Salt and powdered black pepper, as desired
- ❖ 30 millilitres (2 tablespoons) olive oil
- ❖ 40 grams (2 cups) fresh parsley leaves, cut up
- ❖ 15 grams (2 tablespoons) capers, liquid removed
- ❖ 2 Serrano peppers, seeded and finely cut up

Directions:

1. For preheating: set your oven at 205 °C (400 °F).
2. Rub the sardines with salt and pepper lightly.
3. In a large-sized ovenproof wok, sizzle the oil on burner at around medium heat.
4. Cook the sardines for around 3 minutes.
5. Flip the sardines and blend in remnant ingredients.
6. Immediately, shift the wok into oven and bake for around 5 minutes.
7. Enjoy hot.

Lemony Sole

Servings | 4   Time | 25 minutes
Nutritional Content (per serving):
Cal | 291   Fat | 18.8g   Protein | 28g   Carbs | 2.8g   Fibre | 1g

Ingredients:

- ❖ Olive oil baking spray
- ❖ 30 millilitres (2 tablespoons) lemon juice
- ❖ Salt, as desired
- ❖ Powdered black pepper, as desired
- ❖ 2 green onions, sliced
- ❖ ½ lemon, thinly sliced

- ❖ 90 millilitres (1/3 cup) extra-virgin olive oil
- ❖ 5 grams (1 teaspoon) dry oregano
- ❖ 455 grams (1 pound) sole fillets
- ❖ 4 cloves garlic, finely cut up
- ❖ 5 grams (¼ cup) fresh parsley, cut up

Directions:

1. For preheating: set your oven at 180 °C (350 °F).
2. Spray a baking pan with baking spray.
3. For the oil mixture: in a small-sized basin, whisk all together lemon juice, olive oil, oregano and a pinch of salt.
4. Reserve half of oil mixture in your refrigerator.
5. Rub the fish fillets with a bit of salt and pepper.
6. Lay down the fish fillets into the baking pan and top with garlic.
7. Lay down the green onion around the fish fillets.
8. Put the remnant oil mixture on top of fish fillets, followed by parsley and lemon slices.
9. Bake in your oven for around 10-15 minutes.
10. Enjoy hot.

Cod in Lemon Butter Sauce

Servings | 2   Time | 25 minutes
Nutritional Content (per serving):
Cal | 301   Fat | 18.9g   Protein | 31.1g   Carbs | 2.5g   Fibre | 0.3g

Ingredients:

- 2 (150-gram) (6-ounce) cod fillets
- Salt and powdered black pepper, as desired
- 2 cloves garlic, finely cut up
- 5 grams (2 teaspoons) fresh dill weed
- 5 grams (1 teaspoon) onion powder
- 45 grams (3 tablespoons) butter, divided
- 1-2 lemon slices

Directions:

1. Rub each cod fillet with onion powder, salt and pepper.
2. In a medium-sized cast-iron wok, sizzle 15 grams of butter on burner at around high heat.
3. Cook the cod fillets for around 4-5 minutes from both sides.
4. Shift the cod fillets onto a plate.
5. Meanwhile, in a frying pan, melt the remnant butter over low heat.
6. Cook the garlic and lemon slices for around 40-60 seconds.
7. Blend in cooked cod fillets and dill and cook with a cover for around 1-2 minutes.
8. Take off the cod fillets from burner and shift onto the serving plates.
9. Top with the pan sauce and enjoy immediately.

Cod with Tomatoes & Olives

Servings | 4   Time | 30 minutes
Nutritional Content (per serving):
Cal | 230   Fat | 9.9g   Protein | 21.8g   Carbs | 10.2g   Fibre | 2.9g

Ingredients:

- ❖ 30 millilitres (2 tablespoons) olive oil
- ❖ 1 onion, sliced thinly
- ❖ 5 grams (1 tablespoon) fresh parsley, cut up
- ❖ 1 (400-gram) (14-ounce) can diced tomatoes

- ❖ 2 cloves garlic, finely cut up
- ❖ 120 millilitres (½ cup) dry white wine
- ❖ 90 grams (½ cup) black olives, pitted and sliced
- ❖ 455 grams (1 pound) cod fillets

Directions:

1. In a large-sized wok, sizzle oil on burner at around heat.
2. Cook the garlic and onion for around 4-5 minutes.
3. Blend in remnant ingredients except for cod fillets.
4. Cook for around 5 minutes.
5. Blend in cod fillets and cook for 5 minutes.
6. Enjoy hot.

Tomato-Braised Cod

Servings | 5   Time | 50 minutes
Nutritional Content (per serving):
Cal | 248   Fat | 8.1g   Protein | 33.1g   Carbs | 12.9g   Fibre | 3.2g

Ingredients:

- ❖ 5 grams (1 teaspoon) dried dill weed
- ❖ 10 grams (2 teaspoons) ground coriander
- ❖ 5 grams (1 teaspoon) ground turmeric
- ❖ 1 large-sized onion, cut up
- ❖ 2 jalapeño peppers, cut up
- ❖ 55 grams (3 tablespoons) tomato paste
- ❖ 120 millilitres (½ cup) water

- ❖ 10 grams (2 teaspoons) sumac
- ❖ 5 grams (1 teaspoon) ground cumin
- ❖ 30 millilitres (2 tablespoons) olive oil
- ❖ 8 cloves garlic, cut up
- ❖ 5 medium-sized tomatoes, cut up
- ❖ 30 millilitres (2 tablespoons) lemon juice
- ❖ 5 (150-gram) (6-ounce) cod fillets

Directions:

1. For the spice mixture: in a small-sized basin, put in dill weed and spices and blend to incorporate.
2. In a large-sized, deep wok, sizzle the oil on burner at around medium-high heat.
3. Cook the onion for around 2 minutes.
4. Put in garlic and jalapeño and cook for around 2 minutes.
5. Blend in tomatoes, tomato paste, lemon juice, water, half of the spice mixture, salt and pepper.
6. Cook the mixture until boiling.
7. Immediately turn down the heat at around medium-low.
8. Cook with a cover for around 10 minutes, mixing time to time.
9. Meanwhile, rub the cod fillets with the remnant spice mixture, salt and pepper.
10. Lay out the fish fillets into the wok and gently, press into the tomato mixture.
11. Immediately turn up the heat at around medium-high.
12. Cook for around 2 minutes.
13. Immediately turn down the heat at around medium.
14. Cook with a cover for around 10-15 minutes.
15. Enjoy hot.

Cod & Veggies Bake

Servings | 4   Time | 35 minutes
Nutritional Content (per serving):
Cal | 139   Fat | 20.5g   Protein | 27.3g   Carbs | 5.4g   Fibre | 2.3g

Ingredients:

- Olive oil baking spray
- 60 grams (½ cup) onion, finely cut up
- 1 clove garlic, finely cut up
- 400 grams (2 cups) fresh tomatoes, cut up
- 4 (150-gram) (6-ounce) cod steaks

- 5 millilitres (1 teaspoon) olive oil
- 115 grams (1 cup) courgette, cut up
- 5 grams (2 tablespoons) fresh basil, cut up
- Salt and powdered black pepper, as needed
- 40 grams (1/3 cup) feta cheese, crumbled

Directions:

1. For preheating: set your oven at 230 °C (450 °F).
2. Spray a large-sized shallow baking pan with baking spray.
3. In a wok, sizzle the oil on burner at around medium heat.
4. Cook the onion, courgette and garlic for around 4-5 minutes.
5. Blend in basil, tomatoes, salt, and pepper and immediately Take off from burner.
6. Lay out the cod steaks into baking pan and top with the tomato mixture.
7. Sprinkle with the feta cheese.
8. Bake in your oven for around 15 minutes.
9. Enjoy hot.

Salmon with Dill Sauce

Servings | 2   Time | 35 minutes
Nutritional Content (per serving):
Cal | 351   Fat | 24.7g   Protein | 33.2g   Carbs | 0.9g   Fibre | 0.5g

Ingredients:

- ❖ 5 grams (¼ cup) fresh dill, cut up and divided
- ❖ 2½ grams (½ teaspoon) fennel seeds, crushed lightly
- ❖ 15 millilitres (1 tablespoon) lemon juice
- ❖ 30 millilitres (2 tablespoons) olive oil
- ❖ 5 grams (1 teaspoon) lemon zest
- ❖ 2½ grams (½ teaspoon) smoked paprika
- ❖ Salt and powdered black pepper, as needed
- ❖ 2 (150-gram) (6-ounce) skin-on salmon fillets

Directions:

1. In a basin, put in half of dill, lemon zest, paprika, fennel seeds, salt and pepper and blend to incorporate.
2. Rub the salmon fillets with dill mixture and then drizzle with lemon juice.
3. In a large-sized wok, sizzle the oil on burner at around medium heat..
4. Lay out the salmon fillets into the wok and immediately turn down the heat at around the low.
5. Cook for around 20 minutes.
6. Change the side of fish and cook for around 5 minutes more.
7. With a frying ladle, shift the salmon fillets onto a plate-lined with kitchen towels.
8. Enjoy immediately with the decoration of remnant dill.

Stuffed Salmon

Servings | 4   Time | 30 minutes
Nutritional Content (per serving):
Cal | 345   Fat | 16.3g   Protein | 47.1g   Carbs | 4.4g   Fibre | 1.1g

Ingredients:

- 120 grams (4 cups) fresh spinach, cut up
- 55 grams (½ cup) oil-packed sun-dried tomatoes, liquid removed and cut up
- 4 (225-gram) (8-ounce) salmon fillets
- Salt and powdered black pepper, as desired
- 85 grams (½ cup) artichoke hearts, liquid removed and cut up
- 30 grams (¼ cup) feta cheese, crumbled
- Pinch of garlic powder

Directions:

1. In a large-sized saucepan of lightly salted boiling water, cook the spinach for around 40 seconds.
2. In a colander, drain the spinach and immediately immerse in a basin of ice water.
3. Again, drain the spinach thoroughly and shift into a basin.
4. In the basin of spinach, put in artichokes, sun-dried tomatoes and feta cheese and blend to incorporate.
5. With a knife, make a horizontal cut in the center of each salmon fillet. (Do not cut all the way through).
6. Rub each salmon fillet with garlic powder, salt, and pepper.
7. Stuff each salmon pocket with spinach mixture.
8. Sizzle a cast-iron wok on burner at around medium heat.
9. In the wok, put in salmon fillets, skin-sides down and cook for around 5 minutes.
10. Change the side of fillets and cook for around 5 minutes.
11. Again change the side of fillets and cook for around 5 minutes.
12. Enjoy hot.

Tilapia & Tomato Bake

Servings | 4   Time | 25 minutes
Nutritional Content (per serving):
Cal | 246   Fat | 7.4g   Protein | 37.2g   Carbs | 9.4g   Fibre | 2.7g

Ingredients:

- ❖ 2 (400-gram) (14-ounce) cans diced tomatoes with basil and garlic with juice
- ❖ 1¼ grams (¼ teaspoon) dried oregano
- ❖ 4 (150-gram) (6-ounce) tilapia fillets
- ❖ 75 grams (2/3 cup) feta cheese, crumbled

- ❖ 10 grams (1/3 cup) fresh parsley, cut up and divided
- ❖ 2½ grams (½ teaspoon) red pepper flakes
- ❖ 30 millilitres (2 tablespoons) lemon juice

Directions:

1. For preheating: set your oven at 205 °C (400 °F).
2. In a shallow baking pan, put in tomatoes, half of parsley, oregano and red pepper flakes and blend to incorporate thoroughly.
3. Lay out the tilapia fillets over the tomato mixture and drizzle with the lemon juice.
4. Place some tomato mixture over the tilapia fillets and sprinkle with the feta cheese.
5. Bake in your oven for around 12-14 minutes.
6. Enjoy hot with the decoration of remnant parsley.
7.

Halibut Parcel

Servings | 4   Time | 50 minutes
Nutritional Content (per serving):
Cal | 365   Fat | 20.7g   Protein | 37.2g   Carbs | 8.2g   Fibre | 2.6g

Ingredients:

- ❖ 1 onion, cut up
- ❖ 1 (140-gram) (5-ounce) jar pitted Kalamata olives
- ❖ 15 millilitres (1 tablespoon) lemon juice
- ❖ 4 (150-gram) (6-ounce) halibut fillets
- ❖ 1 large-sized tomato, cut up

- ❖ 30 grams (¼ cup) capers
- ❖ 60 millilitres (¼ cup) olive oil
- ❖ Salt and powdered black pepper, as desired
- ❖ 15 grams (1 tablespoon) Greek seasoning

Directions:

1. For preheating: set your oven at 175 °C (350 °F).
2. In a basin, put in onion, tomato, onion, olives, capers, oil, lemon juice, salt and pepper and blend to incorporate.
3. Rub the halibut fillets with the Greek seasoning.
4. Lay out the halibut fillets onto a large-sized piece of heavy-duty foil.
5. Top the fillets with the tomato mixture.
6. Carefully fold all the edges of to create a large-sized packet.
7. Arrange the packet onto a baking tray.
8. Bake in your oven for around 30-40 minutes.
9. Take off the foil packet from oven and shift onto a platter for around 5 minutes.
10. Carefully unwrap the foil and shift the fish mixture onto serving plates.
11. Enjoy hot.

Halibut & Olives Bake

Servings | 4   Time | 20 minutes
Nutritional Content (per serving):
Cal | 306   Fat | 11.6g   Protein | 43.7g   Carbs | 5.7g   Fibre | 1.6g

Ingredients:

❖ 1   ❖ 1

- Olive oil baking spray
- 4 (150-gram) (6-ounce) haddock fillets
- 30 millilitres (2 tablespoons) olive oil
- Salt and powdered black pepper, as desired
- 1 small-sized capsicum, seeded and cut into thin strips
- ½ small onion, thinly sliced
- 45 grams (¼ cup) pitted Greek olives, sliced
- 1 (225-gram) (8-ounce) can tomato sauce
- 30 grams (¼ cup) feta cheese, crumbled

Directions:

1. For preheating: set your oven at 205 °C (400 °F).
2. Spray a baking pan with baking spray.
3. Lay down the haddock into the baking pan.
4. Brush the fish fillets with oil and then dust with salt and pepper.
5. Lay out the capsicum, onion and olives on top of fish fillets followed by tomato sauce and cheese.
6. Bake in your oven for around 15-20 minutes.
7. Enjoy hot.

Tuna with Olives

Servings | 4   Time | 40 minutes
Nutritional Content (per serving):
Cal | 665   Fat | 39g   Protein | 69.3g   Carbs | 8.5g   Fibre | 2.8g

Ingredients:

- 90 millilitres (1/3 cup) olive oil
- 3 cloves garlic, finely cut up and divided
- 8 fresh basil leaves, cut up
- 4 (225-gram) (8-ounce) tuna steaks
- 180 grams (1 cup) black olives, pitted and sliced
- 1 large-sized onion, cut up
- 200 grams (1 cup) Roma tomato, cut up
- 10 grams (¼ cup) fresh parsley, cut up and divided
- Salt and powdered black pepper, as desired
- 15 grams (4 teaspoons) capers, rinsed

Directions:

1. In a large-sized anti-sticking wok, sizzle 45 millilitres of olive oil on burner at around medium heat.
2. Cook the onion for around 3 minutes.
3. Put in 2 cloves garlic and cook for around 2 minutes.
4. Blend in tomatoes, basil and half of parsley and cook for around 15 minutes, mixing time to time.
5. Meanwhile, rub the tuna steaks with salt and pepper.
6. In another large-sized wok, sizzle the remnant olive oil on burner at around medium heat.
7. Cook the remnant garlic for around 1 minute.
8. In the wok, put in tuna steaks and immediately turn up the heat at around medium-high.
9. Cook for around 2 minutes, mixing time to time.
10. Lay out the tomato mixture, olives and capers over tuna steaks and gently blend to incorporate.
11. Immediately turn down the heat at around low.
12. Cook for around 5 minutes.
13. Decorate with remnant parsley and enjoy.

Tuna in Wine Sauce

Servings|4 Time|25 minutes
Nutritional Content (per serving):
Cal| 334   Fat| 11.2g   Protein| 41g   Carbs| 7.3g   Fibre| 2.3g

Ingredients:

- Olive oil baking spray
- 30 millilitres (2 tablespoons) olive oil, divided
- 200 grams (1 cup) fresh tomatoes, cut up
- 125 grams (2/3 cup) olives, pitted and sliced
- 5 grams (1 tablespoon) lemon zest, grated
- 5 grams (3 tablespoons) fresh parsley, cut up

- 4 (150-gram) (6-ounce) tuna steaks
- Salt and powdered black pepper, as desired
- 2 garlic cloves, finely cut up
- 240 millilitres (1 cup) dry white wine
- 30 grams (¼ cup) capers, liquid removed
- 5 grams (2 tablespoons) fresh thyme, cut up
- 30 millilitres (2 tablespoons) lemon juice

Directions:

1. For preheating: set your grill to high heat.
2. Spray the grill grate with baking spray.
3. Coat the tuna steaks with 15 millilitres of oil and sprinkle with salt and pepper.
4. Put it aside for around 5 minutes.
5. For sauce: in a small-sized wok, sizzle the remnant oil on burner at around medium heat.
6. Cook the garlic for around 1 minute.
7. Put in tomatoes and cook for around 2 minutes.
8. Blend in wine.
9. Cook the mixture until boiling.
10. Put in remnant ingredients except for parsley and cook for around 5 minutes.
11. Blend in parsley, salt and pepper and take off from burner.
12. Meanwhile, lay out the tuna steaks onto your grill over direct heat.
13. Cook for around 1-2 minutes from both sides.
14. Enjoy the tuna steaks hot with the topping of sauce.

Octopus & Potato Stew

Servings|8   Time|2 hours 55 minutes
Nutritional Content (per serving):
Cal| 602   Fat| 9.6g   Protein| 75.2g   Carbs| 48.2g   Fibre| 5.8g

Ingredients:

- ❖ 2 kilograms (4¼ pounds) octopus, washed
- ❖ 5 bay leaves, divided
- ❖ 2 onions, cut up
- ❖ 4 tomatoes, cut up
- ❖ 2 bay leaves
- ❖ 4 large-sized potatoes, cut into chunks
- ❖ Salt and powdered black pepper, as desired
- ❖ 1 onion, halved
- ❖ 30 millilitres (2 tablespoons) olive oil
- ❖ 5 cloves garlic, sliced
- ❖ 15 grams (1 tablespoon) paprika
- ❖ 150 millilitres (½ cup plus 2 tablespoons) white wine

Directions:

1. Take off the eyes of the octopus and cut out the beak.
2. Then, clean the head thoroughly.
3. In a large-sized saucepan of water, put in octopus, halved onion and 3 bay leaves.
4. Cook for around 45-60 minutes.
5. Drain the octopus, reserving 960 millilitres (4 cups) of the cooking liquid.
6. In a large-sized saucepan, sizzle the oil on burner at around medium heat.
7. Cook the cut up onions and garlic for around 4-5 minutes.
8. Put in tomatoes and paprika and cook for around 5 minutes, mixing time to time.
9. Put in white wine and 2 bay leaves and cook for around 3-5 minutes.
10. Blend in reserved cooking liquid and cook for around 1 hour.
11. Meanwhile, cut the cooked octopus into bite-sized pieces.
12. In the pot of tomato mixture, blend in octopus pieces and potatoes.
13. Cook for around 20 minutes.
14. Blend in salt and pepper and enjoy hot.

Octopus in Tomato Sauce

Servings | 8   Time | 1 hour 40 minutes
Nutritional Content (per serving):
Cal | 319   Fat | 10.1g   Protein | 38.4g   Carbs | 13.8g   Fibre | 1.3g

Ingredients:

- 1 kilogram (2¼ pounds) fresh octopus, washed
- 60 millilitres (¼ cup) olive oil
- Pinch of saffron threads, crushed
- 20 grams (1 tablespoon) tomato paste
- 20 grams (1 tablespoon) honey
- 180 millilitres (¾ cup) red wine
- 5 grams (¼ cup) fresh basil leaves, cut up

- 1 bay leaf
- 90 millilitres (1/3 cup) water
- 2 onions, finely cut up
- 1 clove garlic, finely cut up
- 1 (400-gram) (14-ounce) can diced tomatoes
- Salt and powdered black pepper, as desired

Directions:

1. Take off the eyes of the octopus and cut out the beak.
2. Then, clean the head thoroughly.
3. In a large-sized, deep saucepan, put in octopus, bay leaf and water on burner at around medium heat.
4. Cook for around 20 minutes.
5. Put in wine and cook for around 50 minutes.
6. Meanwhile, for the sauce: in a wok, sizzle the oil on burner at around medium heat.
7. Cook the onions and saffron for around 3-4 minutes.
8. Put in garlic and tomato paste and cook for around 1-2 minutes.
9. Blend in tomatoes and honey and cook for around 10 minutes.
10. Shift the sauce into the pan of octopus and cooking for around 15 minutes.
11. Enjoy hot with the decoration of basil.

Vegetarian Recipes

Lemony Potatoes

Servings | 6   Time | 10 minutes
Nutritional Content (per serving):
Cal | 198   Fat | 8.9g   Protein | 3.1g   Carbs | 25.9g   Fibre | 4.4g

Ingredients:

- ❖ 60 millilitres (¼ cup) olive oil
- ❖ 60 millilitres (¼ cup) vegetable broth
- ❖ 5 grams (1 tablespoon) dried rosemary
- ❖ 5 cloves garlic, finely cut up
- ❖ 60 millilitres (¼ cup) lemon juice
- ❖ 5 grams (1 tablespoon) dried oregano
- ❖ 955 grams (2 pounds) potatoes, cut into

Directions:

1. For preheating: set your oven at 220 °C (425 °F).
2. In a large-sized roasting pan, put in oil, lemon juice, broth, dried herbs, salt and pepper and blend to incorporate.
3. Put in potatoes and blend with oil mixture.
4. Bake in your oven for around 20 minutes.
5. Take out the roasting pan from oven and sprinkle the potatoes with garlic.
6. Change the side of potatoes.
7. Bake in your oven for around 20 minutes.
8. Enjoy hot.

Green Beans with Potatoes

Servings | 6   Time | 1¼ hours
Nutritional Content (per serving):
Cal | 203   Fat | 9.1g   Protein | 5.2g   Carbs | 29.2g   Fibre | 8.3g

Ingredients:

- 60 millilitres (¼ cup) olive oil
- 5 cloves garlic, finely cut up
- 5 grams (1 teaspoon) ground cumin
- 240 millilitres (1 cup) water
- 1 bay leaf
- 455 grams (1 pound) potatoes, cut into small piece
- 30 millilitres (2 tablespoons) lemon juice

- 1 large-sized onion, finely cut up
- 5 grams (1 teaspoon) dried oregano
- 1 (800-gram) (28-ounce) can peeled whole tomatoes
- 680 grams (1½ pounds) fresh green beans, fat removed and cut up
- Salt and powdered black pepper, as desired
- 10 grams (½ cup) fresh parsley, cut up

Directions:

1. For preheating: set your oven at 150 °C (300 °F).
2. In a large-sized Dutch oven, sizzle the oil on burner at around medium heat.
3. Cook the onions for around 5 minutes.
4. Put in garlic, cumin, and oregano.
5. Cook for around 2 mins, mixing all the time.
6. Blend in tomatoes, beans, potatoes, water, bay leaf, salt and pepper and immediately turn up the heat to high.
7. Cook the mixture until boiling.
8. Cook for around 15 minutes, mixing time to time.
9. Cover the Dutch oven and shift into your oven.
10. Bake for around 35 minutes.
11. Take off the pot from oven and blend in lemon juice and parsley.
12. Enjoy hot.

Capsicum & Potato Bake

Servings|6   Time|1 hour 20 minutes
Nutritional Content (per serving):
Cal| 227   Fat| 12.4g   Protein| 4.1g   Carbs| 28g   Fibre| 4.5g

Ingredients:

- Olive oil baking spray
- 45 millilitres (3 tablespoons) olive oil
- 30 millilitres (2 tablespoons) lemon juice
- 10 grams (¾ cup) fresh coriander, cut up
- 2½ grams (½ teaspoon) ground cumin
- 1¼ grams (¼ teaspoon) cayenne pepper powder
- 3 large-sized capsicums, seeded and cut into pieces
- 4 celery stalks, cut up
- 30 millilitres (2 tablespoons) olive oil
- 6 cloves garlic, cut up
- 45 millilitres (3 tablespoons) red wine vinegar
- 10 grams (¾ cup) fresh parsley, cut up
- 10 grams (2 teaspoons) paprika
- Salt, as desired
- 680 grams (1½ pounds) red potatoes, scrubbed and cut into slices
- 455 grams (1 pound) tomatoes, cut into 8 wedge

Directions:

1. For preheating: set your oven at 175 ℃ (350 °F).
2. Spray a large-sized shallow baking pan with baking spray.
3. For sauce: in a food mixer, put in oil, oi, vinegar, lemon juice, fresh herbs, spices and salt and process to form a smooth mixture.
4. In a large-sized basin, put in all vegetables and herb sauce and toss it all together to blend.
5. Shift the potato mixture into baking pan and drizzle with the oil.
6. With a piece of heavy-duty foil, cover the baking pan.
7. Bake in your oven for around 35 minutes.
8. Take off the foil and bake in your oven for around 20-30 minutes.
9. Enjoy hot.

Potato & Olives Stew

Servings | 6   Time | 1 hour
Nutritional Content (per serving):
Cal | 259   Fat | 13.4g   Protein | 3.9g   Carbs | 33.6g   Fibre | 6.1g

Ingredients:

- 90 millilitres (1/3 cup) olive oil
- 135 grams (¾ cup) kalamata olives, pitted
- 2 cloves garlic, finely cut up
- 5 grams (1 teaspoon) dried oregano
- Salt and powdered black pepper, as desired
- 680 grams (2½ pounds) potatoes, peel removed and cubed
- 300 grams (1½ cups) tomatoes, cut up
- Warm water, as desired

Directions:

1. In a large-sized wok, sizzle the oil on burner at around medium heat.
2. Blend in potatoes, olives and garlic and cook for 3-5 minutes.
3. Blend in tomatoes and oregano.
4. Blend in enough water to cover the potatoes.
5. Cook the mixture until boiling.
6. Immediately turn down the heat to low.
7. Cook with a cover for around 30 minutes.
8. Blend in salt and pepper and enjoy hot

Veggie Stew

Servings | 6   Time | 40 minutes
Nutritional Content (per serving):
Cal | 168   Fat | 8.7g   Protein | 6g   Carbs | 14.8g   Fibre | 3.1g

Ingredients:

- ❖ 45 millilitres (3 tablespoons) olive oil
- ❖ 2 capsicums, seeded and sliced
- ❖ 4 cloves garlic, finely cut up
- ❖ 10 green olives, pitted and sliced
- ❖ 480 millilitres (2 cups) vegetable broth
- ❖ Salt and powdered black pepper, as desired
- ❖ 455 grams (1 pound) fresh mushroom
- ❖ 1 onion, cut up
- ❖ 180 millilitres (¾ cup) red wine
- ❖ 150 grams (6 ounces) tomato paste
- ❖ 2 bay leaves

Directions:

1. In a large-sized pan, sizzle the oil on burner at around medium-high heat.
2. Cook the mushrooms, capsicums, onions and garlic for around 2-3 minutes.
3. Put in red wine and scrape up the brown bits.
4. Cook for around 2-3 minutes.
5. Blend in olives, tomato paste, broth and bay leaves.
6. Cook the mixture until boiling.
7. Immediately turn down the heat at around low.
8. Cook with a cover for around 20 minutes.
9. Blend in salt and pepper and enjoy hot.

Stuffed Grape Leaves

Servings | 10   Time | 20 minutes
Nutritional Content (per serving):
Cal | 161   Fat | 12.4g   Protein | 3.6g   Carbs | 12.1g   Fibre | 2.8g

Ingredients:

- ❖ 135 grams (¾ cup) kalamata olives, pitted and cut up
- ❖ 55 grams (½ cup) Gorgonzola cheese, crumbled
- ❖ 1 capsicum, seeded and cut up
- ❖ 5 grams (¼ cup) fresh basil leaves, cut up
- ❖ 1 (225-gram) (8-ounce) jar grape leaves packed in brine

- ❖ 135 grams (¾ cup) green olives, pitted and cut up
- ❖ 95 grams (¾ cup) macadamia nuts, cut up
- ❖ 4 tomatoes, seeded and cut up
- ❖ 4 cloves garlic, cut up
- ❖ 20 grams (2 tablespoons) brown sugar
- ❖ Salt and powdered black pepper, as desired

Directions:

1. In a large-sized basin, put in olives, Gorgonzola cheese, macadamia nuts, tomatoes, capsicum, garlic, basil, brown sugar, salt and pepper and blend to incorporate.
2. Lay down the grape leaves onto a smooth counter.
3. Lay out a heaped tablespoonful of olive mixture in the center of each leaf.
4. Roll each leaf around the olives mixture.
5. Arrange the rolls onto large-sized baking tray and shift into your refrigerator to chill thoroughly before enjoying.

Chickpea Gyros

Servings | 4   Time | 35 minutes
Nutritional Content (per serving):
Cal | 344   Fat | 6.7g   Protein | 11.2g   Carbs | 60.4g   Fibre | 7.1g

Ingredients:

- ❖ Olive oil baking spray
- ❖ 15 millilitres (1 tablespoon) olive oil
- ❖ 15 grams (1 tablespoon) paprika
- ❖ Salt and powdered black pepper, as desired
- ❖ 4 pita breads
- ❖ ¼ onion cut into strips
- ❖ 2 lettuce leaves, roughly cut up

- ❖ 1 (425-gram) (15-ounce) can chickpeas, liquid removed
- ❖ 2½ grams (½ teaspoon) cayenne pepper powder
- ❖ 255 grams (1 cup) tzatziki sauce
- ❖ 1 tomato, sliced

Directions:

1. For preheating: set your oven at 205 °C (400 °F).
2. Spray a large-sized rimmed baking tray with baking spray.
3. With paper towel, pat dry the chickpeas thoroughly.
4. In a large-sized basin, put in chickpeas, oil, paprika, cayenne pepper, salt and pepper and blend to incorporate.
5. Lay out the chickpeas onto the baking tray.
6. Roast in your oven for around 20 minutes.
7. Take off the baking tray from oven and let them cool slightly.
8. Lay out the pita breads onto a smooth surface.
9. Spread tzatziki onto one side of each pita and then to each with chickpeas, followed by onion, tomato and lettuce.
10. Fold each pita in half and enjoy.

Spinach Pie

Servings | 8 Time | 1½ hours
Nutritional Content (per serving):
Cal | 556   Fat | 36.4g   Protein | 19.6g   Carbs | 40.2g   Fibre | 4.2g

Ingredients:

- ❖ Olive oil baking spray
- ❖ 45 millilitres (3 tablespoons) olive oil
- ❖ 225 grams (½ pound) fresh mushrooms, sliced
- ❖ 2 eggs, whisked
- ❖ 1 (455-gram) (16-ounce) package phyllo dough

- ❖ 955 grams (2 pounds) spinach, cut up
- ❖ 1 onion, cut up
- ❖ 440 grams (2 cups) ricotta cheese
- ❖ 110 grams (1 cup) feta cheese
- ❖ 5 grams (2 tablespoons) dried basil
- ❖ 170 grams (¾ cup) butter, liquefied

Directions:

1. For preheating: set your oven at 190 °C (375 °F).
2. Spray a deep pie plate with baking spray.
3. In a large-sized saucepan of boiling water, cook the spinach for around 2-3 minutes.
4. Drain the spinach and put it aside.
5. In a medium-sized wok, sizzle the oil on burner at around medium heat.
6. Cook the onions and mushrooms for around 5-7 minutes.
7. Blend in spinach and immediately take off from burner.
8. In a medium-sized basin, put in ricotta, feta, eggs and basil and blend to incorporate.
9. Lay out a phyllo sheet on the bottom of pie plate and brush with melted butter.
10. Lay out 5-6 phyllo sheets in the same manner.
11. Spread the ricotta mixture over the phyllo sheets.
12. Lay out more 5-6 phyllo sheets in the same manner.
13. Spread spinach mixture over the phyllo sheets.
14. Lay out more 5-6 phyllo sheets in the same manner.
15. Trim the extra edges of dough.
16. Bake in your oven for around 1 hour.
17. Enjoy warm.

Beans in Tomato Sauce

Servings|4   Time|2 hours 5 minutes
Nutritional Content (per serving):
Cal| 249   Fat| 11.8g   Protein| 8.5g   Carbs| 31.2g   Fibre| 7.9g

Ingredients:

- 360 grams (2 cups) dry butter beans
- 1 small-sized onion, finely cut up
- 5 grams (1 teaspoon) ground cinnamon
- 20 grams (1 tablespoon) tomato paste
- 20 grams (1 tablespoon) tomato paste
- 5 grams (1 teaspoon) dried oregano

- 45 millilitres (3 tablespoons) olive oil
- 3 cloves garlic, finely cut up
- 2 (400-gram) (14-ounce) cans diced tomatoes
- 10 grams (2 teaspoons) brown sugar
- Salt and powdered black pepper, as desired

Directions:

1. In a large-sized basin of water, soak the beans for all the night.
2. Drain the beans and then rinse well.
3. In a medium-sized saucepan of boiling water, put in beans.
4. Cook the mixture until boiling.
5. Cook with a cover for around 45 minutes.
6. For preheating: set your oven at 180 °C (355 °F).
7. Meanwhile, in a large-sized wok, sizzle the oil on burner at around medium heat.
8. Cook the onion for around 3-4 minutes.
9. Put in garlic and cook for around 1 minute.
10. Immediately turn down the heat to low and blend in cinnamon.
11. Cook for around 1 minute.
12. Blend in tomatoes, tomato paste, brown sugar, oregano, salt and pepper.
13. Cook for around 30 minutes.
14. Drain the beans, reserving about 120 millilitres of cooking water.
15. Put the beans and reserved cooking water into the pan of tomatoes and blend thoroughly.
16. Shift the blended mixture into a large-sized casserole dish.
17. Bake in your oven for around 1 hour.
18. Enjoy hot.

Pasta & Veggie Bake

Servings|4 Time|40 minutes
Nutritional Content (per serving):
Cal| 421   Fat| 23.8g   Protein| 15.6g   Carbs| 37.9g   Fibre| 1.9g

Ingredients:

- 170 grams (1 cup) artichoke hearts
- 110 grams (1 cup) olive oil-packed sun-dried tomatoes
- 5 grams (1 teaspoon) fresh rosemary, finely cut up
- Salt and powdered black pepper, as desired
- 455 grams (1 pound) cooked spaghetti

- 180 grams (1 cup) green olives, pitted
- 4 cloves garlic, sliced thinly
- 90 millilitres (1/3 cup) extra-virgin olive oil
- 1¼ grams (¼ teaspoon) dried oregano
- 1¼ grams (¼ teaspoon) dried thyme
- 455 grams (1 pound) feta cheese block

Directions:

1. For preheating: set your oven at 175 °C (350 °F).
2. In a large-sized basin, blend all together the artichokes, olives and sun-dried tomatoes.
3. In another small basin, put in oil, herbs, salt and pepper and blend to incorporate.
4. In a baking pan, put in feta block.
5. Arrange the artichoke mixture around the feta block.
6. Pour the oil mixture over feta and veggies.
7. Bake in your oven for around 20 minutes.
8. Now set the oven to broiler and broil for around 1-2 minutes.
9. Divide the spaghetti onto serving plates.
10. Top each plate with feta and veggie mixture and enjoy.

Salad Recipes

Watermelon & Cucumber Salad

Servings | 8   Time | 15 minutes
Nutritional Content (per serving):
Cal | 148   Fat | 4.2g   Protein | 3.4g   Carbs | 27.7g   Fibre | 1.5g

Ingredients:

- ❖ 30 millilitres (2 tablespoons) lemon juice
- ❖ 15 millilitres (1 tablespoon) olive oil
- ❖ 1 (2275-gram) (5-pound) watermelon, peel removed and cut into cubes
- ❖ 55 grams (½ cup) feta cheese, crumbled
- ❖ 35 grams (2 tablespoons) honey
- ❖ Pinch of salt
- ❖ 360 grams (3 cups) cucumber, cubed
- ❖ 5 grams (¼ cup) fresh mint leaves, torn

Directions:

1. For vinaigrette: in a small-sized basin, put in lemon juice, oil, honey and salt and whisk to incorporate thoroughly.
2. For salad: in a large-sized salad basin, blend all together watermelon, cucumber and mint.
3. Place the vinaigrette over watermelon mixture and toss it all to mingle nicely.
4. Top with the feta cheese and enjoy immediately.

Fig & Onion Salad

Servings | 2   Time | 15 minutes
Nutritional Content (per serving):
Cal | 202   Fat | 12.1g   Protein | 5.6g   Carbs | 21.1g   Fibre | 7.6g

Ingredients:

- ❖ 30 millilitres (2 tablespoons) olive oil
- ❖ 30 grams (2 tablespoons) tahini
- ❖ 5 grams (1 teaspoon) Dijon mustard
- ❖ 120 grams (4 cups) fresh spinach
- ❖ 25 grams (¼ cup) unsweetened coconut, shredded

- ❖ 30 millilitres (2 tablespoons) lemon juice
- ❖ 5 grams (1 teaspoon) maple syrup
- ❖ Salt and ground black pepper, as desired
- ❖ 10 fresh figs, halved
- ❖ 120 grams (1 cup) onion, sliced

Directions:

1. For the dressing: in a small-sized basin, put in oil, vinegar, tahini, maple syrup, mustard, salt and pepper and whisk to incorporate thoroughly.
2. In a salad dish, put in remnant ingredients and blend.
3. Place dressing over salad and toss all together to mingle nicely.
4. Enjoy immediately.

Cucumber & Olives Salad

Servings|6   Time|15 minutes
Nutritional Content (per serving):
Cal| 189   Fat| 15.3g   Protein| 5.3g   Carbs| 10.3g   Fibre| 2.4g

Ingredients:

- ❖ 2 cucumbers, peel removed and cut up
- ❖ 90 grams (½ cup) black olives, pitted and sliced
- ❖ 60 millilitres (¼ cup) olive oil
- ❖ Salt and powdered black pepper, as desired
- ❖ 3 large ripe tomatoes, cut up
- ❖ 1 small-sized onion, cut up
- ❖ 20 millilitres (4 teaspoons) lemon juice
- ❖ 1½ grams (½ teaspoon) dried oregano
- ❖ 110 grams (1 cup) feta cheese, crumbled

Directions:

1. In a large-sized serving dish, put in cucumbers and remnant ingredients except feta and toss it all to mingle nicely.
2. Top with feta and enjoy immediately.

Mixed Veggie Salad

Servings | 6   Time | 15 minutes
Nutritional Content (per serving):
Cal | 275   Fat | 23.2g   Protein | 7.1g   Carbs | 14.3g   Fibre | 5.6g

Ingredients:

- ❖ 2 cucumbers, peel removed and cut up
- ❖ 180 grams (1 cup) Kalamata olives, pitted
- ❖ 240 grams (8 cups) fresh baby spinach
- ❖ 60 millilitres (¼ cup) extra-virgin olive oil
- ❖ 5 grams (1 teaspoon) dried oregano
- ❖ 110 grams (1 cup) feta cheese, crumbled
- ❖ 3 large Roma tomatoes, cut up
- ❖ 1 large-sized avocado, peel removed, pitted and cut up
- ❖ 30 millilitres (2 tablespoons) lemon juice
- ❖ Salt and powdered black pepper, as desired

Directions:

1. In a large-sized serving basin, put in cucumbers and remnant ingredients except feta and toss it all to mingle nicely.
2. Top with the feta and enjoy immediately.

Chickpeas Salad

Servings|6   Time|15 minutes
Nutritional Content (per serving):
Cal| 288   Fat| 11.6g   Protein| 8.7g   Carbs| 40g   Fibre| 8.8g

Ingredients:

- 60 millilitres 60 millilitres (¼ cup) extra-virgin olive oil
- 1 clove garlic, finely cut up
- 5 grams (1 teaspoon) ground sumac
- Salt and powdered black pepper, as desired
- 500 grams (2½ cups) tomatoes, cut up
- 240 grams (2 cups) cucumber, cut up
- 1 onion, cut up
- 10 grams (½ cup) fresh parsley leaves, cut up

- 30 millilitres (2 tablespoons) lemon juice
- 30 millilitres (2 tablespoons) white wine vinegar
- 2½ grams (½ teaspoon) red pepper flakes
- 2 (425-gram) (15-ounce) cans chickpeas, liquid removed
- 90 grams (½ cup) Kalamata olives, pitted
- 10 grams (½ cup) fresh mint leaves, cut up

Directions:

1. For the dressing: in a small-sized basin, put in oil, lemon juice, vinegar, garlic, sumac, red pepper flakes, salt and pepper and whisk to incorporate thoroughly.
2. For the salad: in a large-sized serving dish, put in remnant ingredients and blend.
3. Place the dressing over the salad and toss it all to mingle nicely.
3. Put it aside for around 30 minutes.
4. Lightly blend the salad and enjoy.

Orzo & Veggie Salad

Servings | 2 Time | 10 minutes
Nutritional Content (per serving):
Cal | 340   Fat | 25.1g   Protein | 7.9g   Carbs | 25.2g   Fibre | 4.4g

Ingredients:

- ❖ 100 grams (½ cup) uncooked whole-wheat orzo pasta
- ❖ 5 grams (1 tablespoon) fresh parsley, finely cut up
- ❖ Salt and powdered black pepper, as desired
- ❖ 180 grams (1 cup) black olives, pitted and sliced
- ❖ 3 green onions, cut up

- ❖ 90 millilitres (1/3 cup) olive oil
- ❖ 20 millilitres (4 teaspoons) lemon juice
- ❖ 5 grams (2 teaspoons) lemon zest, grated
- ❖ 3 plum tomatoes, cut up
- ❖ 180 grams 6 cups fresh spinach, cut up roughly
- ❖ 55 grams (½ cup) feta cheese, crumbled

Directions:

1. For the salad: in a large-sized pan of the salted boiling water, cook the orzo for around 8-10 minutes.
2. Drain the orzo and rinse well.
3. In a large-sized salad dish, put in pasta and put it aside to cool.
4. For the dressing: in a small-sized basin, put in oil, lemon juice, zest, salt and pepper and whisk to incorporate thoroughly.
5. In the dish of pasta, put in remnant ingredients.
6. Place the dressing over salad and toss it all to mingle nicely.
7. Shift into your refrigerator to chill thoroughly before serving.

Rice & Veggie Salad

Servings | 8   Time | 35 minutes
Nutritional Content (per serving):
Cal | 275   Fat | 13.7g   Protein | 6g   Carbs | 32.7g   Fibre | 1.6g

Ingredients:

- ❖ 600 millilitres (2½ cups) water
- ❖ Salt, as desired
- ❖ 60 millilitres (¼ cup) lemon juice
- ❖ 5 grams (1 teaspoon) fresh oregano, finely cut up
- ❖ 60 grams (2 cups) fresh spinach leaves, cut up
- ❖ 50 grams (½ cup) green onion, cut up
- ❖ 90 grams (½ cup) Kalamata olives, pitted and sliced

- ❖ 285 grams (1½ cups) white rice, rinsed
- ❖ 90 millilitres (1/3 cup) extra-virgin olive oil
- ❖ 1 clove garlic, finely cut up
- ❖ 1¼ grams (¼ teaspoon) red pepper flakes
- ❖ Powdered black pepper, as desired
- ❖ 1 capsicum, seeded and finely cut up
- ❖ 1 small-sized cucumber, peel removed, seeded and finely cut up
- ❖ 110 grams (1 cup) feta cheese, crumbled

Directions:

1. In a medium-sized saucepan, put in water on burner at around medium-high heat.
2. Cook the water until boiling.
3. Put in rice and salt and blend to incorporate.
4. Immediately turn down the heat low.
5. Cook with a cover for around 15 minutes.
6. Take off from burner and put it aside with a cover for around 5 minutes.
7. Take off the cover and with a fork, fluff the rice.
8. Put it aside to cool slightly.
9. For dressing: in a large-sized basin, put in oil, lemon juice, garlic, oregano, red pepper flakes, salt and pepper and whisk to incorporate thoroughly.
10. In the basin of dressing, put in rice and toss it all to mingle nicely.
11. Put in spinach and toss to coat.
12. Put it aside for around 20 minutes.
13. In the basin of rice mixture, put in remnant ingredients and toss it all to mingle nicely.
14. Enjoy immediately.

Chicken & Veggies Salad

Servings | 6   Time | 20 minutes
Nutritional Content (per serving):
Cal | 252   Fat | 15.7g   Protein | 22.9g   Carbs | 5.3g   Fibre | 1.7g

Ingredients:

- ❖ 60 millilitres (¼ cup) olive oil
- ❖ 5 grams (1 tablespoon) fresh coriander, finely cut up
- ❖ 180 grams (1 cup) Kalamata olives, pitted
- ❖ 55 grams (½ cup) feta cheese, crumbled
- ❖ 30 millilitres (2 tablespoons) lemon juice
- ❖ Salt and powdered black pepper, as desired
- ❖ 420 grams (3 cups) cooked chicken
- ❖ 60 grams (½ cup) onion, finely cut up

Directions:

1. For the dressing: in a small-sized basin, put in oil, lemon juice, coriander, salt and pepper and whisk to incorporate thoroughly.
2. For salad: in a large-sized salad basin, blend all together the remnant ingredients.
3. Place dressing over salad and toss it all to mingle nicely.
4. Shift into your refrigerator to chill thoroughly before serving.

Steak & Olives Salad

Servings | 6   Time | 30 minutes
Nutritional Content (per serving):
Cal | 598   Fat | 44.7g   Protein | 45.8g   Carbs | 5.3g   Fibre | 2.6g

Ingredients:

- Olive oil baking spray
- Salt and powdered black pepper, as desired
- 90 millilitres (1/3 cup) olive oil, divided
- 30 grams (2 tablespoons) plain Greek yogurt
- 2 large-sized green chilies, finely cut up
- Salt and powdered black pepper, as desired
- 5 grams (2 tablespoons) lemon zest, grated
- 5 grams (2 tablespoons) fresh mint, cut up
- 680 grams (1½ pounds) aged rump steak, fat removed
- 65 grams (½ cup) mayonnaise
- 5 grams (1 teaspoon) Dijon mustard
- 15 millilitres (1 tablespoon) lemon juice
- 10 anchovies, cut up
- 540 grams (3 cups) green olives, pitted and sliced
- 5 grams (2 tablespoons) fresh parsley, cut up

Directions:

1. For preheating: set your grill to medium-high heat.
2. Spray the grill grate with baking spray.
3. Sprinkle the beef steak with salt and pepper and then drizzle with 30 millilitres of oil.
4. Place the steak onto your grill and cook for around 5 minutes from both sides.
5. Take off the steak from grill and place onto a chopping block for around 10 minutes before slicing.
6. Cut the steak into serving-sized portions diagonally across the grain.
7. For the dressing: in a medium-sized basin, put in mayonnaise, yogurt, mustard, lemon juice, green chilies anchovies, salt and pepper and blend to incorporate.
8. Put in steak slices and blend to incorporate.
9. For salad: in another small-sized basin, put in olives, lemon zest and herbs and mix.
10. Divide the steak mixture onto serving plates and top with the olives mixture.
11. Drizzle with remnant oil and enjoy.

Tuna Salad

Servings | 6   Time | 20 minutes
Nutritional Content (per serving):
Cal | 280   Fat | 18.6g   Protein | 21.3g   Carbs | 9g   Fibre | 2.6g

Ingredients:

- ❖ 90 millilitres (1/3 cup) olive oil
- ❖ 10 grams (2 teaspoons) Dijon mustard
- ❖ 5 grams (1 teaspoon) lemon zest, grated
- ❖ 1 onion, cut up
- ❖ 2 cucumbers, sliced
- ❖ 90 grams (½ cup) Kalamata olives, pitted
- ❖ 5 grams (¼ cup) fresh basil leaves

- ❖ 45 millilitres (3 tablespoons) lemon juice
- ❖ Salt and powdered black pepper, as desired
- ❖ 3 (140-gram) (5-ounce) cans tuna in olive oil
- ❖ 1 large-sized tomato, sliced
- ❖ 240 grams (8 cups) fresh spinach leaves, torn

Directions:

1. For the vinaigrette: in a basin, put in oil, lemon juice, mustard, zest, salt and pepper and whisk to incorporate thoroughly.
2. For the salad: in a large-sized serving basin, put in remnant ingredients and mix.
3. Place the vinaigrette over the salad and toss all together to mingle nicely.
4. Shift into your refrigerator with a cover for around 30-40 minutes before enjoying.

Soup Recipes

Tomato & Feta Soup

Servings | 3   Time | 1¼ hours
Nutritional Content (per serving):
Cal | 365   Fat | 26.8g   Protein | 12.7g   Carbs | 22.4g   Fibre | 3.5g

Ingredients:

- ❖ 700 grams (4 cups) cherry tomatoes
- ❖ 3 cloves garlic, smashed
- ❖ 1¼ grams (¼ teaspoon) red pepper flakes
- ❖ Salt and powdered black pepper, as desired
- ❖ 2 white bread slices, crusts removed and cut into cubes
- ❖ 2 shallots, roughly cut up
- ❖ 80 millilitres (¼ cup plus 4 teaspoons) olive oil, divided
- ❖ 115 grams (4 ounces) feta cheese, crumbled
- ❖ 480 millilitres (2 cups) l chicken broth

Directions:

1. For preheating: set your oven at 205 °C (400 °F).
2. In a medium-sized baking pan, put in tomatoes, shallots, garlic, 60 millilitres of oil, red pepper flakes, salt and pepper and toss to combine.
3. Then arrange the tomato mixture in an even layer.
4. Place 2/3 of the feta into the center of the tomato mixture.
5. Drizzle the top of feta with 10 millilitres of oil.
6. Bake in your oven for around 40-45 minutes.
7. Meanwhile, in a small-sized baking pan, put in bread cubes, remnant oil and (¼ teaspoon) of salt and toss to combine. Put it aside.
8. Take off the baking pan of tomato mixture from burner.
9. Again, set the temperature of your oven to 190 ℃ (375 °F).
10. Bake in your oven for around 15 minutes, tossing once after 8 minutes.
11. Meanwhile, in a clean blender, put in tomato mixture and 60 millilitres of chicken broth and process until smooth.
12. Shift the blended mixture into a medium-sized saucepan and blend in remnant broth.
13. Place the saucepan of tomato mixture on burner at around medium-high heat and bring it to a boil.
14. Immediately turn down the heat at around medium-low.
15. Cook for around 10 minutes.
16. Enjoy the soup hot with the decoration of croutons.

Tomato & Orzo Soup

Servings | 6   Time | 40 minutes
Nutritional Content (per serving):
Cal | 229   Fat | 10.4g   Protein | 6g   Carbs | 30.2g   Fibre | 3.4g

Ingredients:

- 60 millilitres (¼ cup) olive oil
- 4 cloves garlic, grated
- 850 grams (30 ounces) canned tomatoes, pureed
- 5 grams (1 teaspoon) granulated sugar
- 1440 millilitres (6 cups) water
- 5 grams (1 teaspoon) fresh mint, finely cut up

- 1 onion, finely cut up
- 20 grams (1 tablespoon) tomato paste
- 5 grams (1 teaspoon) dried oregano
- 1¼ grams (¼ teaspoon) red pepper flakes
- Salt and powdered black pepper, as desired
- 200 grams (1 cup) uncooked orzo pasta
- 30 grams (¼ cup) feta cheese, crumbled

Directions:

1. In a large-sized soup pan, sizzle oil on burner at around medium heat.
2. Cook the onion for around 10 minutes, mixing time to time.
3. Cook the garlic for around 20-30 seconds.
4. Blend in tomato paste and cook for around 20-30 seconds.
5. Blend in pureed tomatoes, sugar, oregano, a red pepper flakes, salt and pepper.
6. Cook the mixture until boiling.
7. Put in orzo pasta and cook for around 8-10 minutes, mixing time to time.
8. Blend in mint and enjoy hot with the decoration of feta.

Dill Veggie Soup

Servings | 6   Time | 45 minutes
Nutritional Content (per serving):
Cal | 190   Fat | 6.5g   Protein | 8.7g   Carbs | 26.5g   Fibre | 4.7g

Ingredients:

- ❖ 30 millilitres (2 tablespoons) olive oil
- ❖ 2 carrots, peel removed and cut up
- ❖ 1440 millilitres (6 cups) chicken broth
- ❖ Salt and powdered black pepper, as desired

- ❖ 1 large-sized onion, cut up
- ❖ 3 potatoes, peel removed and cubed
- ❖ 20 grams (1 cup) fresh dill, cut up

Directions:

1. In a large-sized soup pan, sizzle oil on burner at around medium heat.
2. Cook the onions for around 5 minutes.
3. Blend in carrots and potatoes and cook for around 3-5 minutes.
4. Blend in chicken broth.
5. Cook the mixture until boiling.
6. Immediately turn down the heat to low.
7. Cook with a cover for around20 minutes.
8. Blend in dill, salt and pepper and cook for around 5 minutes.
9. Enjoy hot.

Beans Soup

Servings | 6 Time | 35 minutes
Nutritional Content (per serving):
Cal | 185   Fat | 2.9g   Protein | 11.6g   Carbs | 27.33g   Fibre | 12.4g

Ingredients:

- 15 millilitres (1 tablespoon) olive oil
- 1 onion, cut up
- 1¼ grams (¼ teaspoon) dried thyme
- 480 millilitres (2 cups) vegetable broth
- 480 millilitres (2 cups) water
- Salt and powdered black pepper, as desired
- 1 celery stalk, cut up
- 1 garlic clove, minced
- 2 (455-gram) (16-ounce) cans cannellini beans, liquid removed
- 90 grams (3 cups) fresh spinach, cut up
- 15 millilitres (1 tablespoon) lemon juice

Directions:

1. In a large soup pan, sizzle oil on burner at around medium heat.
2. Cook the celery and onion for around 3-4 minutes.
3. Put in garlic and thyme and cook for around 1 minute.
4. Blend in beans, broth and water.
5. Cook the mixture until boiling.
6. Immediately turn down the heat to low.
7. Cook for around 15 minutes.
8. Take off from heat and with a flying ladle, shift 2 cups of beans mixture into a bowl.
9. Set aside to cool slightly.
10. In a high-power mixer, put in slightly cooled bean mixture and process to form a smooth mixture.
11. Return the pureed mixture into the soup and blend to incorporate.
12. Lay out the soup pan on burner at around medium heat.
13. Blend in spinach, salt and pepper and cook for around 3-4 minutes.
14. Blend in lemon juice and enjoy hot.

Lemon Chicken Soup

Servings | 6   Time | 50 minutes
Nutritional Content (per serving):
Cal | 335   Fat | 10.3g   Protein | 28g   Carbs | 30.3g   Fibre | 1.7g

Ingredients:

- ❖ 30 millilitres (2 tablespoons) olive oil
- ❖ 2 celery stalks, finely cut up
- ❖ 100 grams (1 cup) green onion, finely cut up
- ❖ 2 bay leaves
- ❖ Salt and powdered black pepper, as desired
- ❖ 120 millilitres (½ cup) lemon juice
- ❖ 5 grams (3 tablespoons) fresh parsley, cut up

- ❖ 1 large-sized carrots, peel removed and finely cut up
- ❖ 2 cloves garlic, finely cut up
- ❖ 1920 millilitres (8 cups) chicken broth
- ❖ 190 grams (1 cup) rice, rinsed
- ❖ 340 grams (12 ounces) cooked chicken, shredded
- ❖ 2 large-sized eggs

Directions:

1. In a large-sized Dutch oven, sizzle 15 millilitres of oil on burner at around medium-high heat.
2. Cook the carrots, celery and green onions for around 3-4 minutes.
3. Blend in garlic and cook for around 1 minute.
4. Put in broth and bay leaves and immediately turn up the heat to high.
5. Cook the mixture until boiling.
6. Blend in rice, salt and pepper and immediately turn down the heat to medium-low.
7. Cook for around 20 minutes.
8. Blend in cooked chicken and cook for around 5 minutes.
9. Meanwhile, in a medium-sized basin, whisk all together the lemon juice and eggs.
10. While whisking, put in 2 ladles of broth and blend to incorporate.
11. Shift the egg mixture into the soup pan and blend to incorporate.
12. Immediately take off from burner and enjoy hot with a decoration of parsley.

Chicken & Orzo Soup

Servings|8   Time|35 minutes
Nutritional Content (per serving):
Cal| 298   Fat| 10.1g   Protein| 31.4g   Carbs| 17.4g   Fibre| 0.6g

Ingredients:

- 15 millilitres (1 tablespoon) olive oil
- 15 grams (1 tablespoon) Greek seasoning
- 4 green onions, thinly sliced
- 60 millilitres (¼ cup) white wine
- 30 grams (¼ cup) sun-dried tomatoes, cut up
- 5 grams (2 teaspoons) fresh oregano, finely cut up
- 1680 millilitres (7 cups) chicken broth
- 300 grams (1½ cups) uncooked orzo pasta
- 30 millilitres (2 tablespoons) lemon juice
- 680 grams (1½ pounds) boneless chicken breasts, cubed
- 1 clove garlic, finely cut up
- 45 grams (¼ cup) Greek olives, pitted and sliced
- 5 grams (1 tablespoon) capers, liquid removed
- 5 grams (2 teaspoons) fresh basil, finely cut up
- 5 grams (2 teaspoons) fresh parsley, finely cut up

Directions:

1. In a Dutch oven, sizzle the oil on burner at around medium heat.
2. Sear the chicken breasts with Greek seasoning and pepper for around 4-5 minutes.
3. With a frying ladle, shift the chicken breasts onto a plate and put it aside.
4. In the same pan, put in green onions and garlic and cook for around 1 minute.
5. Put in wine and cook for around 1 minute, mixing all the time.
6. Blend in cooked chicken, olives, tomatoes, capers, oregano, basil and broth.
7. Cook the mixture until boiling.
8. Immediately turn down the heat at around low.
9. Cook with a cover for around 15 minutes.
10. Immediately turn up the heat at around medium.
11. Cook the mixture until boiling.
12. Blend in orzo and cook for around 8-10 minutes.
13. Blend in lemon juice and parsley and enjoy hot.

Beef, Lentil & Potato Soup

Servings | 8   Time | 2¼ hours
Nutritional Content (per serving):
Cal | 367   Fat | 7.7g   Protein | 31.1g   Carbs | 43.1g   Fibre | 9.5g

Ingredients:

- 30 millilitres (2 tablespoons) olive oil
- Salt and powdered black pepper, as desired
- 1 large-sized carrot, peel removed and cut up
- 6 cloves garlic, cut up
- 5 grams (1 teaspoon) dried oregano
- 1920-2160 millilitres (8-9 cups) chicken broth
- 5 grams (¼ cup) fresh parsley, cut up
- 455 grams (1 pound) beef chuck, fat removed and cut into cubes
- 1 large-sized celery stalk, cut up
- 1 large-sized onion, cut up
- 5 grams (1 teaspoon) dried rosemary
- 2 large-sized potatoes, peel removed
- 800 grams (4 cups) tomatoes, cut up
- 420 grams (2 cups) dry lentils

Directions:

1. Rub the beef cubes with salt and pepper.
2. In a large-sized soup pan, sizzle the oil on burner at around medium-high heat.
3. Cook the beef cubes for around 8 minutes.
4. With a frying ladle, shift the beef into a basin and put it aside.
5. In the same pan, put in carrot, celery onion, garlic and dried herbs on burner at around medium heat.
6. Cook for around 5 minutes.
7. Blend in potatoes and cook for around 4-5 minutes.
8. Blend in cooked beef, tomatoes and broth and immediately turn up the heat at around high.
9. Cook the mixture until boiling.
10. Immediately turn down the heat low and cook with a cover for around 1 hour.
11. Put in lentils and cook with a cover for around 40 minutes.
12. Blend in salt and pepper and take off from burner.
13. Enjoy hot with the decoration of parsley.

Lamb Soup

Servings | 8   Time | 2½ hours
Nutritional Content (per serving):
Cal | 537   Fat | 15g   Protein | 51g   Carbs | 49.9g   Fibre | 6.1g

Ingredients:

- 910 grams (2 pounds) boneless lamb shoulder, cubed
- 1 onion, cut up
- 35 grams (2 tablespoons) tomato paste
- 5 grams (1 teaspoon) ground cumin
- 1440 millilitres (6 cups) chicken broth
- 2 (400-gram) (14-ounce) cans brown lentils, liquid removed
- 10 grams (½ cup0 fresh parsley, cut up

- Salt and powdered black pepper, as desired
- 30 millilitres (2 tablespoons) olive oil
- 2 cloves garlic, cut up
- 10 grams (2 teaspoons) sweet paprika
- 2 (400-gram) (14-ounce) cans diced tomatoes with juice
- 2 (400-gram) (14-ounce) cans chickpeas, liquid removed

Directions:

1. Rub the lamb cubes with salt and pepper.
2. In a large-sized saucepan, sizzle the oil on burner at around medium-high heat.
3. Sear the lamb cubes in 2 batches for around 4-5 minutes.
4. With a frying ladle, shift the lamb cubes into a bowl.
5. In the same pan, put in onion and garlic on burner at around medium heat.
6. Cook for around 3-4 minutes.
7. Put in cooked lamb, tomato paste and spices and cook for around 1 minute.
8. Blend in the tomatoes and broth.
9. Cook the mixture until boiling.
10. Immediately turn down the heat to low.
11. Cook with a cover for around 1 hour.
12. Blend in the lentils and chickpeas and cook with a cover for around 30 minutes.
13. Take off the cover and cook for around 30 minutes.
14. Blend in the salt and black pepper and enjoy hot with a decoration of parsley.

Cod & Potato Soup

Servings | 5 Time | 35 minutes
Nutritional Content (per serving):
Cal | 288   Fat | 7.6g   Protein | 31.7g   Carbs | 22.3g   Fibre | 4g

Ingredients:

- ❖ 30 millilitres (2 tablespoons) olive oil
- ❖ 1 large-sized onion, cut up
- ❖ 35 grams (2 tablespoons) tomato paste
- ❖ 600 grams(3 cups) potatoes, peel removed and cut up
- ❖ 720 millilitres (3 cups) fish broth
- ❖ 570 grams (1¼ pounds) cod, cut into small chunks
- ❖ Salt and powdered black pepper, as desired
- ❖ 2 celery stalks, cut up
- ❖ 2 cloves garlic, finely cut up
- ❖ 5 grams (1 teaspoon) dried thyme
- ❖ 1 (400gram) (14-ounce can) diced tomatoes with liquid
- ❖ 240 millilitres (1 cup) water
- ❖ 5 grams (3 tablespoons) fresh parsley, cut up

Directions:

1. In a large-sized soup pan, sizzle oil on burner at around medium-high heat.
2. Cook celery and onion for around 4-5 minutes.
3. Blend in garlic, tomato paste and thyme and cook for around 2-3 minutes.
4. Blend in potatoes, tomatoes with juice, broth and water.
5. Cook the mixture until boiling.
6. Immediately turn down the heat at around low.
7. Cook for around 10-12 minutes.
8. Blend in cod and cook for around 4-5 minutes.
9. Blend in salt, pepper and parsley and enjoy hot.

Dessert Recipes

Rice Pudding

Servings | 6   Time | 50 minutes
Nutritional Content (per serving):
Cal | 135   Fat | 3.3g   Protein | 3.7g   Carbs | 22.4g   Fibre | 0.2g

Ingredients:

- ❖ 480 millilitres (2 cups) water
- ❖ 600 millilitres (2½ cups) whole milk, divided
- ❖ 30 grams (¼ cup) cornstarch
- ❖ 1¼ grams (¼ teaspoon) ground cinnamon
- ❖ 95 grams (½ cup) short-grain white rice, rinsed
- ❖ 50 grams (¼ cup) white sugar
- ❖ 5 millilitres (1 teaspoon) vanilla extract

Directions:

1. In a large-sized saucepan, put in water and rice.
2. Cook the mixture until boiling.
3. Immediately turn down the heat at around medium-low.
4. Cook for around 30 minutes.
5. Blend in 480 millilitres of milk and sugar.
6. Immediately turn up the heat at around high.
7. Cook the mixture until boiling.
8. Meanwhile, in a small-sized bowl, blend all together the remnant milk and cornstarch.
9. In the pot of rice mixture, put in the cornstarch mixture and vanilla and blend to incorporate thoroughly.
10.
11. Take off the pot of rice mixture from burner.
12. Shift the pudding into serving dishes and sprinkle with cinnamon.
13. Put them aside for around 30 minutes.
14. Then shift the dishes into your refrigerator for at least 4 hours before enjoying.

Baklava

Servings | 18   Time | 1 hour 5 minutes
Nutritional Content (per serving):
Cal | 392   Fat | 25.9g   Protein | 5.9g   Carbs | 37.9g   Fibre | 2g

Ingredients:

- ❖ Olive oil baking spray
- ❖ 5 grams (1 teaspoon) ground cinnamon
- ❖ 1 (455-gram) (16-ounce) package phyllo dough
- ❖ 240 millilitres (1 cup) water
- ❖ 5 millilitres (1 teaspoon) vanilla extract

- ❖ 455 grams (1 pound) mixed nuts (pistachios, almonds, walnuts), cut up
- ❖ 225 grams (1 cup) butter, liquefied
- ❖ 200 grams (1 cup) white sugar
- ❖ 150 grams (½ cup) honey

Directions:

1. For preheating: set your oven at 175 °C (350 °F).
2. Spray a 23x33-centimetre (9x13-inch) baking pan with baking spray.
3. In a medium-sized basin, put in nuts and cinnamon and toss it all to mingle nicely. Put it aside.
4. Unroll the phyllo dough and cut in half.
5. Arrange 2 dough sheets into baking pan and blend with some butter.
6. Repeat with 8 dough sheets in layers and sprinkle with 2-(3 tablespoons) of nut mixture.
7. Repeat with remnant dough sheets, butter and nuts.
8. Divide into diamond shapes all the way to the bottom of the baking pan.
9. Bake in your oven for around 50 minutes.
10. Meanwhile, for sauce: in a saucepan, put in sugar and water and cook until Sugar is melted, mixing all the time.
11. Blend in honey and vanilla extract and cook for around 20 minutes.
12. Take off the baklava from oven and immediately place the sauce on top.
13. Put it aside to cool before enjoying.

Almond Cookies

Servings | 15   Time | 30 minutes
Nutritional Content (per serving):
Cal | 212   Fat | 13.8g   Protein | 6.9g   Carbs | 16.3g   Fibre | .2g

Ingredients:

- ❖ 300 grams (3 cups) almond flour
- ❖ 5 grams (1 tablespoon) orange zest
- ❖ 3 large-sized egg whites, lightly whisked
- ❖ 150 grams (¾ cup) granulated sugar
- ❖ 1¼ grams (¼ teaspoon) salt
- ❖ 100 grams (1 cup) almonds, cut up

Directions:

1. Lay out the racks to the upper and lower thirds of oven.
2. For preheating: set your oven at 175 °C (350 °F).
3. Lay out bakery paper onto two baking trays.
4. In a large-sized basin, blend all together the almond flour, sugar, orange zest and salt.
5. Put in whisked egg whites and blend to form a dough.
6. With a cookie scooper, divide the dough into balls.
7. Coat the dough balls with cut up almonds.
8. Lay out the cookies onto the baking trays and flatten each slightly.
9. Lay out the baking trays in the upper and lower thirds of the oven.
10. Bake for around 13-15 minutes, rotating the pans from top to bottom after 7 minutes of cooking.
11. Take off from oven and shift the baking pans onto a counter to cool for around 5 minutes.
12. Take off the cookies from baking trays and shift onto a large-sized platter to cool thoroughly before enjoying.

No-Bake Lemon Cheesecake

Servings | 12   Time | 20 minutes
Nutritional Content (per serving):
Cal | 455   Fat | 32.1g   Protein | 8.3g   Carbs | 39.8g   Fibre | 3.6g

Ingredients:

- ❖ Olive oil baking spray
- ❖ 140 grams (1 cup) raw almonds
- ❖ 455 grams (3½ cups) cashews, soaked for all the night
- ❖ 5 grams (2 tablespoons) lemon rind, grated finely
- ❖ 10 drops liquid stevia
- ❖ Salt, as desired

- ❖ 145 grams (1 cup) dates, pitted and cut up
- ❖ 20 grams (3 tablespoons) unsweetened coconut, shredded
- ❖ 100 germs (½ cup) coconut oil, liquefied
- ❖ 180 millilitres (¾ cup) lemon juice
- ❖ 225 grams (¾ cup) maple syrup
- ❖ 5 millilitres (1 teaspoon) vanilla extract

Directions:

1. Spray a springform pan with baking spray.
2. For the crust: in a food mixer, put in dates, almonds, and coconut and process until mixture just starts to combine.
3. Shift the blended mixture into springform pan and, with the back of a spatula, smooth the surface of the crust.
4. For filling: in the clean food mixer, put in cashews and oil and process to incorporate thoroughly
5. Put in remnant ingredients except for lemon slices and process until creamy and smooth.
6. Pour the blended mixture over crust and with the back of a spatula, smooth the top.
7. Shift into your refrigerator for around 1 hour.
8. Cut into 12 portions and enjoy.

Yogurt Cheesecake

Servings|12   Time|1½ hours
Nutritional Content (per serving):
Cal| 305   Fat| 20.7g   Protein| 7.2g   Carbs| 22.8g   Fibre| 0.3g

Ingredients:

- 180 grams (1½ cups) graham cracker crumbs
- 155 grams (1 tablespoon plus 2/3 cup) granulated sugar, divided
- 190 grams (1¾ cups) plain Greek yogurt
- 5 millilitres (1 teaspoon) vanilla extract
- 70 grams (5 tablespoons) unsalted butter, liquefied
- 2 (225-gram) (8-ounce) blocks cream cheese, softened
- 3 large-sized eggs
- 10 millilitres (2 teaspoons) lemon juice

Directions:

1. For preheating: set your oven at 175 °C (350 °F).
2. For crust: in a medium-sized basin, put in graham cracker crumbs, liquefied butter and 15 grams of sugar and bend to incorporate thoroughly.
3. Place the blended mixture into a springform pan and with your hands, press the blended mixture in the bottom and up sides.
4. Bake in your oven for around 8 minutes.
5. Take off the pan of crust from oven and put it aside to cool.
6. Now set the temperature of your oven to 165 °C (325 °F).
7. For filling: attach a stand mixer with paddle attachment.
8. In the basin of mixer, put in cream cheese and whisk to form a smooth mixture.
9. Put in sugar, yogurt, vanilla extract and lemon juice and whisk to form a smooth mixture.
10. Put in eggs one at a time and mix on medium-low speed until just blended.
11. With a large-sized piece of heavy-duty foil, wrap the outer bottom of pan with crust tightly.
12. In a roasting pan, put in around 2½-centimeters (1-inch) of hot water.
13. Lay out the filling mixture over the crust.
14. Lay out the pan of cheesecake into the roasting pan.
15. Bake in your oven for around 45-55 minutes.
16. Turn off the oven and immediately prop the oven door open.
17. Let the cheesecake stay in the oven for around 1 hour.
18. Take off the springform pan from oven and place onto a cooling rack to cool.
19. Now, shift into your refrigerator for around 8 hours before enjoying.

White Chocolate Raspberry Cheesecake

Servings|12   Time|1 hour 40 minutes
Nutritional Content (per serving):
Cal| 491   Fat| 38.2g   Protein| 7.1g   Carbs| 32.5g   Fibre| 0.6g

Ingredients:

- Olive oil baking spray
- 4 (225-gram) (8-ounce) packages cream cheese, softened
- 2½ millilitres (½ teaspoon) almond extract
- 210 grams (2/3 cup) raspberry sauce
- 480 grams (2 cups) whipped cream
- 1 chocolate cookie crust
- 130 grams (¾ cup) pure cane sugar
- 10 millilitres (2 teaspoons) vanilla extract
- 4 large-sized egg yolks
- 115 grams (4 ounces) white chocolate curls

Directions:

1. For preheating: set your oven at 175 °C (350 °F).
2. Spray a springform pan with baking spray.
3. Lay out a piece of heavy-duty foil on the outside of pan.
4. Lay out the crust into the springform pan.
5. In a large-sized basin, put in cream cheese, cane sugar, vanilla extract and almond extract and with an electric mixer, whisk to blend thoroughly.
6. Put in egg yolks and whisk to blend thoroughly.
7. Lay out half of the cheese mixture over the crust.
8. Place half of raspberry sauce on top of cream cheese mixture in the shape of dots
9. With a table knife, swirl the sauce into the cream cheese mixture.
10. Repeat with the remaining cream cheese mixture and raspberry sauce.
11. Again, swirl the sauce into the cream cheese mixture.
12. In a roasting pan, pour around 2½-centimeters (1-inch) of hot water.
13. Now, arrange the springform pan in the roasting pan.
14. Bake in your oven for around 80 minutes.
15. Turn the oven off but keep the cheesecake in the oven for around 30-45 minutes, with the oven door open.
16. Take off the cheesecake from oven and put it aside to cool thoroughly.
17. Shift the cheesecake into your refrigerator to chill for all the night.
18. Sprinkle the chocolate over the cheesecake.
19. Fill a bag with whipped cream and pipe all around the edge of the cheesecake.
20. Divide the cheesecake into serving-sized slices and enjoy.

Lemon Ricotta Cake

Servings | 8   Time | 1 hour 10 minutes
Nutritional Content (per serving):
Cal | 118   Fat | 7.1g   Protein | 9.9g   Carbs | 3.5g   Fibre | 0g

Ingredients:

- ❖ Olive oil baking spray
- ❖ 1495 grams (17½ ounces) ricotta cheese
- ❖ 5 grams (2 teaspoons) lemon zest, grated freshly
- ❖ 4 eggs
- ❖ 3-5 packets stevia powder
- ❖ 30 millilitres (2 tablespoons) lemon juice

Directions:

1. For preheating: set your oven at 175 °C (350 °F).
2. Spray a baking pan.
3. In a large-sized basin, put in ricotta cheese and whisk to form a smooth texture.
4. Put in eggs, one at a time and whisk to incorporate thoroughly.
5. Slowly, put in stevia and whisk to incorporate thoroughly.
6. Put in lemon juice and zest and whisk to incorporate thoroughly.
7. Lay out the blended mixture into baking pan
8. Bake in your oven for around 50-55 minutes.
9. Take off from oven and place onto a counter to cool thoroughly
10. Shift into your refrigerator to chill thoroughly before serving.

Fig Cake

Servings|2   Time|1 hour 10 minutes
Nutritional Content (per serving):
Cal| 348   Fat| 1.3g   Protein| 2.4g   Carbs| 90.6g   Fibre| 14g

Ingredients:

- Olive oil baking spray
- 3 grams (¾ teaspoon) baking powder
- Pinch of salt
- 2 large-sized eggs
- 90 millilitres (1/3 cup) milk
- 55 grams (¼ cup) unsalted butter, liquefied
- 285 grams (10 ounces) fresh figs, cut up

- 195 grams (1½ cups) unbleached all-purpose flour
- 5 grams (1 teaspoon) lemon zest, finely grated
- 60 millilitres (¼ cup) olive oil
- 2½ millilitres (½ teaspoon) vanilla extract

Directions:

1. Lay out a rack in the center portion of the oven.
2. For preheating: set your oven at 175 °C (350 °F).
3. Spray a springform pan with baking spray and then dust it with flour lightly.
4. In a large-sized basin, sift all together the flour, baking powder and salt.
5. Put in lemon zest and blend to incorporate.
6. In a separate basin, put in sugar and eggs and with a hand mixer, whisk to form a thick and pale yellow mixture.
7. Put in milk, oil, butter and vanilla extract and whisk to incorporate thoroughly.
8. Put in flour mixture and with a wooden spoon, mix until well blended.
9. Put it aside for around 10 minutes.
10. In the basin of the flour mixture, put in around ¾ of the figs and gently blend to incorporate.
11. Place the blended mixture into pan and bake in your oven for around 15 minutes.
12. Take off from oven and top the cake with the remnant figs.
13. Bake in your oven for around 35-40 minutes.
14. Take off from oven and place the pan onto a counter for around 10 minutes.
15. Carefully take off the cake from the pan and shift onto a platter to cool thoroughly

Dried Fruit Loaf Cake

Servings | 8   Time | 1 hour 20 minutes
Nutritional Content (per serving):
Cal | 140   Fat | 9.1g   Protein | 24.2g   Carbs | 11.4g   Fibre | 1g

Ingredients:

- Olive oil baking spray
- 1 gram (¼ teaspoon) baking soda
- 3 large-sized eggs
- 30 millilitres (2 tablespoons) olive oil
- 75 grams (¼ cup) honey
- 50 grams (1/3 cup) pumpkin seeds
- 65 grams (½ cup) dried cranberries
- 25 grams (¼ cup) almonds, cut up
- 30 grams (¼ cup) arrowroot powder
- 1¼ grams (¼ teaspoon) salt
- 180 grams (¾ cup) creamy almond butter, softened
- 5 millilitres (1 teaspoon) vanilla extract
- 40 grams (1/3 cup) sunflower seeds
- 45 grams (¼ cup) dried apricots, finely cut up

Directions:

1. For preheating: set your oven at 175 °C (350 °F).
2. Lay out a bakery paper into bread loaf pan and then spray it with baking spray.
3. Place arrowroot powder, baking soda, and salt in a large-sized basin and blend to incorporate.
4. In a separate basin, put in eggs, butter, oil, honey and vanilla extract and whisk to blend thoroughly.
5. Put in egg mixture into basin with flour mixture and blend to incorporate thoroughly.
6. Lightly blend in seeds, dried fruit and almonds.
7. Place the blended mixture into loaf pan.
8. Bake in your oven for around 40-50 minutes.
9. Take off the loaf pan from oven and place onto a counter to cool for around 15 minutes.
10. Take off the cake from pan and shift onto a platter to cool thoroughly before enjoying.

Chocolate Cake

Servings | 15   Time | 45 minutes
Nutritional Content (per serving):
Cal | 196   Fat | 1.3g   Protein | 3.7g   Carbs | 47.8g   Fibre | 3.1g

Ingredients:

- ❖ Olive oil baking spray
- ❖ 400 grams (2 cups) sugar
- ❖ 12 grams (3 teaspoons) baking powder
- ❖ 480 millilitres (2 cups) lukewarm water
- ❖ 5 grams (3 teaspoons) orange zest, grated

- ❖ 325 grams (2½ cups) all-purpose flour
- ❖ 180 grams (1½ cups) cocoa powder
- ❖ Pinch of salt
- ❖ 2½ millilitres (½ teaspoon) vanilla extract

Directions:

1. For preheating: set your oven at 170 ℃ (340 ℉).
2. Spray a cake pan with baking spray.
3. In a large-sized basin, blend all together the flour, sugar, cocoa powder, baking powder and salt.
4. Put in water, vanilla and orange zest and whisk to form a smooth mixture.
5. Put the mixture into the cake pan.
6. Bake in your oven for around 30 minutes.
7. Take off the cake pan from oven and place onto a counter to cool for around 15 minutes.
8. Take off the cake from pan and shift onto a platter to cool thoroughly before enjoying.

Printed in Great Britain
by Amazon

25977998R00071